Assertiveness Training

Learn How to Say No and Stop People-Pleasing by Establishing Healthy Boundaries

Richard Banks

Thank You!

Thank you for your purchase.

I am dedicated to making the most enriching and informational content. I hope it meets your expectations and you gain a lot from it.

Your comments and feedback are important to me because they help me to provide the best material possible. So, if you have any questions or concerns, please email me at richardbanks.books@gmail.com.

Again, thank you for your purchase.

INTRODUCTION

"The duty we owe ourselves is greater than that we owe others." — Louisa May Alcott

Congratulations on purchasing *Assertiveness Training: Learn How to Say No and Stop People-Pleasing by Establishing Healthy Boundaries,* and thank you for doing so.

Do you find that you often have a hard time sharing your opinions? Do you tend to simply agree with whatever everybody else has to say? Is it difficult for you to get your work done on time because you're doing things for everybody else? Do you struggle with the simple word "no?" If you're familiar with these problems, you need to learn how to be assertive. If your first thought is, "Well, I don't want to be rude," let me assure you, assertiveness and rudeness aren't the same thing.

Learning how to be more assertive can massively improve your relationships and your overall sense of self-confidence. When you can express yourself assertively and speak up for yourself, other people will respect you more. Even more importantly, you'll respect yourself more. This book will show you how to get more out of your life and feel better about yourself by helping you to become more assertive without coming across as bossy or forceful. Most importantly, this book will demonstrate the vital principle that assertiveness isn't an innate ability. Instead, it's something that can be learned and developed.

We all face challenges with communication. Nobody knows the perfect method of how to clearly communicate with others in a way that's both respectful and specific. Most people fall into one of the two extremes in communication. We're either people-pleasers or aggressive. Unfortunately, neither of these are favorable for effective communication. Now, why is that?

Pinpointing precisely why so many people struggle with communication would be hard to do. We all miscommunicate for our own reasons. It could be something we picked up from our parents or something we developed over the years through our experiences. Whatever the reason, we need to correct this to build healthy relationships.

If an individual tends to keep quiet and is fearful of letting others know their opinion, they often feel invisible in social situations. If you're such a person, you're likely facing difficulties identifying and arranging your priorities. Often, you may agree to what others ask of you, even if that means you have to go through difficulties and put your desires and aspirations on hold for the time being. If you're tired of taking a passive role in relationships and want to learn how to set stronger boundaries so you can take control of your life, this book is for you.

Being assertive isn't the same as being aggressive, which is a distinction that many people struggle with.

We can assert our feelings and thoughts without being intimidating and mean. We're not looking to make other people fear us. We want people to respect us.

I'm here to help you learn assertiveness skills. Through research and personal discovery, I've found some great strategies to take the biggest "people-pleasers" and turn them into assertive people with strong boundaries.

Now, you may be asking why assertiveness is so important. It's important because being assertive is how you get to where you want to be in the world. Assertiveness teaches you the best words, body language, and tone to use to make your point so that others listen. I can recall over the years many conversations in which I was dismissed and disregarded before I started utilizing assertive strategies. At times, people simply ignored everything I said because I was being too passive. My words said, "I want this," but everything else said, "Meh."

Once you learn to stand up for yourself, amazing things will begin to happen in your life. Remember, being assertive doesn't mean being bossy. Rather, it allows you to communicate clearly and fairly with people around you.

This book will be helpful if you're a person who feels like you need to increase your assertiveness, improve your communication skills, deal more effectively with conflict, improve your level of confidence, and be a better leader. It will take time, but I promise that you'll learn how to speak up for yourself in a respectful manner.

However, the only way this will happen is if you take this book to heart and start practicing the techniques we'll cover. It's really that simple. You'll learn how to spot what you've been doing wrong and how to correct those issues.

By the end of this book, you'll be well on your way to changing your life for the better in numerous ways, and you'll be wondering how you ever lived without this information. There's no better time than now to change the parts of yourself that you wish were different, so let's begin!

CHAPTER 1: HOW WE COMMUNICATE

Communication is perhaps the most empowering of all life skills. It enables us to pass information to other people and understand what's said to us. Communication serves five major goals: informing, expressing feelings, imagining, influencing, and meeting social expectations. Each of these goals is reflected in the form of communication. Furthermore, it's a skill you can learn, just like riding a bike or writing. If you're willing to work on this, it can dramatically improve every aspect of your life.

Our lives revolve around the ability to share experiences and information. This process isn't unique to human beings. Animals and plants have their own way of communicating with members of their species, and it's this medium of sharing information and knowledge that allows most species to thrive and survive in their environment.

What Is Communication?

Communication is defined as transferring information to produce greater understanding. It's a process of creating and sharing ideas, information, views, facts, and feelings from one place, person, or group to another.

Communication contains three parts—the sender, the message, and the recipient. The sender will typically "encode" the message with a mixture of non-verbal and verbal communication. They transmit it in some way—usually through speech or writing. The recipient must "decode" the message. The transmission of the message can be affected by several factors that include how the message is delivered along with the location and culture in which it's delivered, and with what emotion. Because of this complexity, it's essential to have good communication skills. This will ensure that the communication is effective, accurate, and unambiguous.

Additionally, you could have multiple recipients, and each recipient can have a slightly different interpretation of the message. Two people can infer two very different messages from the same words and body language. It's even possible that neither of them has the same understanding that the sender meant for the message.

Communication Types

While we can quickly think about communication as a simple transmission of a message between sender and recipient, there's much more to it than that. Communication can range from non-verbal, like the rise of an eyebrow, to verbal, like the change in tone and pitch of our voice. Let's look at the different types of communication before moving into the communication process.

Non-Verbal Communication

Non-verbal communication can be intentional or unintentional. Most of us don't have perfect control over our facial expressions when talking. We've all had the experience of somebody saying something rude to us, and we raised our eyebrows in response. That's an unplanned, automatic reaction to hearing something that alarms us.

Let's look at forms of non-verbal communication.

1. Facial expressions

A person's facial expressions can help us determine if we believe or trust what they're saying. The most trustworthy expression will have a slight smile and a raised eyebrow. This expression shows confidence and friendliness.

We often make judgments about how intelligent someone is by the configuration of their face and their facial expressions. People who have a narrow face and a prominent nose are often thought to be very intelligent. People who smile and have joyous expressions are frequently judged as being more

16

intelligent than a person who looks angry.

Start by looking at the eyes. You can look at the blinking rate, the size of the pupils, and the gaze to learn more about what the person is saying. The light level within the environment can affect pupil dilation, but emotions can also cause changes in pupil size. You might have heard the expression "bedroom eyes." If a person's pupils are dilated, they could be aroused or very interested.

If a person looks at you while talking to you, that usually means they're paying attention and interested in what you're saying. However, prolonged eye contact might feel threatening. Alternatively, breaking eye contact and looking away often could indicate that someone is trying to hide their real feelings or is uncomfortable or distracted.

Mouth movements and expressions are helpful when trying to read body language. Chewing on the lower lip might indicate a person is feeling insecure, fearful, or worried.

If they cover their mouth with their hand, it might indicate they're trying to be polite if they cough or yawn, but it could also be an attempt to cover up disapproval. Smiling is the best body signal, but smiles can be interpreted in several ways. Smiles can be genuine, or they might indicate cynicism, sarcasm, or convey false happiness.

2. Posture

Next, the way person is standing can cue you into hidden meanings behind their message. Pay attention to the upper body, as this is often where defensive signs can be seen. Crossed arms indicate a shield, a resistance to what's being said. If a person stands with their chest thrust outward, it means they want to draw attention to that area. It can also be a romantic display. Women understand that men are programmed to become aroused by breasts. When you notice a woman standing in a way that emphasizes her chest, she may be inviting intimate relations. Men thrust their chest out to show off their chest and possibly to hide their gut. The difference is that men do this to both women and men.

If a person leans forward, it brings them closer to the other person. This can mean one of two things. First, it lets you know they're interested, which could be a simple interest in what's being said, but this movement could also indicate romantic interest.

Second, a lean-forward can invade personal space and therefore be perceived as a threat. This tends to be an aggressive move, and it's often an unconscious gesture that influential people use.

In the lower body, the legs serve as an exclamation point and can let you know what a person is thinking. They can show dominance, and they can let you know if the person is comfortable with you.

Watch the direction of a person's feet to discover where their attention is. Usually, our feet point in the direction of what our mind is paying attention to. Everybody has a lead foot, depending on the dominant hand. When a person that we're interested in is talking, our lead food will point toward them. However, if a person is in a situation that they want to get out of, their foot may point toward the closest exit or in the direction they want to go. You may see a person seated and talking to somebody, but their feet are positioned as if they're standing to leave.

3.   Physical touch and gestures

The human hand has 27 bones, and it's an expressive part of our bodies. Second only to a person's face, the hands are the best source of body language. Gestures of the hands vary significantly across cultures, and one hand gesture might be innocent in one country but offensive in another. Hand signals might be subtle, but they show what our subconscious is thinking. A gesture might be exaggerated and done using both hands to emphasize a point.

Verbal Communication

When speaking, we communicate a lot more than just the words we say. Tone and pitch assists in conveying our message as does how much formality we use in our language. By carefully choosing how we use these aspects, we can ensure that the message is received the way we want it to be.

1.   Pitch

When we speak, our emotions will affect how we say things. When frustrated or angry, the pitch of our voice often rises. This isn't a bad thing, but knowing how to control it can help you communicate effectively with others.

2. Tone

We've all found ourselves in situations that were upsetting or frustrating. Allowing these things to change our tone from professional to rude is a mistake. The tone of our voice influences what the listener hears in our message.

3. Content

Content is the most significant part of verbal communication. The words we choose are important. This is why it's essential to be aware of the formality of your speech. Depending on if you're speaking with your boss or your friend, you'll choose different words.

Written Communication

Being able to communicate through writing effectively is an important skill as well. From text messages to emails, we write every day. In fact, in the past several years, we've grown to rely on written communication more and more. We've also learned how easy it is to misunderstand things in written form.

Unclear messages, incorrect understanding of content or tone, or missing information are problems that happen in written communication. The reader can misread the tone of the message simply because they're having a bad day. If you sense someone has misunderstood a written message—or their response makes it clear that they misunderstood—it's essential to immediately follow up with a verbal chat to sort out the miscommunication. That's the only way for both people to clarify what the message was meant to be and how it was received.

Visual Communication

The last type of communication is visual. This is the most commonly used type of communication because it's become the norm in social media. More people and organizations are turning to this form of communication. There are many different forms of visual communication, including graphs, videos, sketches, photographs, charts, and even GIFs and emojis. Think about how a chart can convey data in a more effective manner than relying on a verbal description.

Communication Process

Now that we know the types of communication, let's get back to the process of communication. A misunderstanding can happen at any point during the communication process. Being able to communicate effectively helps minimize possible misunderstandings and overcome barriers to communication at every step of the process.

The effective communicator will understand who they're talking to (their audience), choose an appropriate form of communication, work on their message, and encode the message with the appropriate verbal and non-verbal information to reduce the chance of misunderstanding. They'll also look to gain feedback from the receiver. Receivers can use reflection and clarification to ensure they correctly understand the message. Preventing misunderstandings doesn't fall solely on the communicator but on the receiver as well.

Here's the basic, step-by-step process of communication:

1. The sender comes up with the message they want to send.
2. They encode their message (with verbal and non-verbal information) and send it through the proper channel.
3. The recipient decodes the message.
4. Once the recipient has decoded the message, they provide the sender with feedback in the form of questions or comments.
5. They encode that feedback and send it through the proper channel.
6. The sender then decodes the recipient's feedback.

The communication channel is the means by which you transmit your message. You could choose to share your message through text, email, face-to-face, radio broadcast, social media, phone call, video, and so on.

The options are many, but picking the appropriate one is important. It will also affect how you encode the message.

When it comes to encoding messages, you have to do so in a way that works with your chosen communication channel. We do this all day, every day, so we already know the basics of how this works. The trick is to remember your channel. A text you write for a report at work wouldn't work well being broadcast on the radio. Also, the abbreviated text for a text message wouldn't be appropriate for a speech or a letter.

How a person decodes a message depends on their understanding and experiences with the context, their psychological state, how they feel, how well they know the sender, and the place and time they receive the message.

The last part of communication is feedback. The recipient lets the sender know they understood and received the message. This feedback is likely to be conveyed through non-verbal and verbal reactions. The sender should pay close attention to this so they know if their message was clearly understood. The extent and form of the feedback will vary depending on the communication channel. If it's a communication sent by voice, whether face-to-face or on the phone, the feedback will be immediate and direct. However, feedback conveyed through radio or television will often be delayed and indirect.

Four Communication Styles

We'll now explore the four communication styles that are predominantly in use. Not everyone uses the same communication style, and that's why you need to be aware of all of them, so you don't face challenges when attempting to communicate with anyone.

Passive Communication

One of the most common styles of communication is being passive. To avoid any kind of conflict or misunderstanding, passive people tend to readily accept anything and everything that other people ask of them. They'd rather please people than make their opinion known.

Trademarks of passive communication include keeping your head down and doing your best to avoid confrontation. It's often a "go with the flow" type of feeling in which a person gives in to the demands and requests of others. They'll always avoid expressing what they want.

If somebody says, "Hey, can you go to the store and grab me some beer?" the passive communicator will reply, "Yeah, no problem," even if it means they'll miss their favorite TV show, or their dinner will get cold.

Being passive doesn't mean you don't say anything. Instead, it just means the person agrees to what someone else says. It may mean a person is passive in what they say, but more often than not, their passivity plays out not in what they say but in doing what they don't want to do to please other people.

The very essence of passive communication is embedded in the ideology of letting the other person win or get what they want without trying even once to stand up for themselves. When someone communicates passively, they forget about themselves in the process. They start neglecting their wishes and desires. Their life belongs to others because all they do is address the wishes and demands of those around them. Someone who communicates passively feels anxious all the time, and they sense their life is out of control. They don't have any control over what happens simply because they're an adjunct to someone else's life and not living their own. The feeling is of being stuck in a void, and often they're engulfed by depression. It's natural for them to feel upset and resentful all the time. It might happen that, after a point, they start resenting themselves because they can't stop being the way they are. They can never find a resolution to their problems, and they're unable to resolve conflict.

OUTCOME: I lose, you win.

Aggressive Communication

On the other end of the spectrum is the aggressive style of communication. In the passive style, you tend to let others have power over you, but in the aggressive style, you try to take control of others. This is the style demonstrated by bullies.

This communication style is born from a place of fear. This person fears they won't be heard or understood and, therefore, they enter into an interaction or conversation with a loud volume to their voice and an attitude of entitlement. They often believe this is the best way to communicate and the only way to get people to listen. They also love to demand things. You might hear, "You better not be fixing meatloaf again. I'll lose my mind if I see that on the table tonight! You better fix something else."

They're also rude and belittling because the more they break others down, the more important they believe they'll feel. A consistently aggressive communication style is nearly always a response to a person feeling threatened or afraid. Bullies behave in this way to feel powerful in an attempt to compensate for the fact that they're bullied at home. Most adults who are aggressive communicators suffer from an innate sense of helplessness.

This communication style can often end up having the exact effect the communicator is trying to avoid—listeners don't hear the content of the sentences because they're distracted by the way the message is being conveyed. When people are faced with an aggressive communication style, they tend to become defensive and closed-off, unwilling to engage any further in the interaction.

Aggressive communication is all about you getting what you want at the expense of everything and everyone else. An aggressive person will never take into consideration what others are feeling or going through. As long as they get what they want, their life is set.

OUTCOME: I win, you lose.

Passive-Aggressive Communication

This communication style combines aspects of passive and aggressive communication. It's typically used to get our way or to express frustration without facing the consequences. Passive-aggressive communicators display an external attitude that their words don't match. They use passive or even submissive body language to appear non-confrontational while communicating with their words in an aggressive manner.

Passive-aggressive communicators tend to speak aggressively to indirectly make a point but act out passively in front of the person. Gossip is a common example. The person wants to undermine someone or vent about what that person did without facing the consequences of saying it to their face. Sarcasm can be a type of passive-aggressive communication if you do to "get a jab in" at the expense of somebody else but not take the blame because you were "just joking." Also, intentionally doing something poorly so you won't get asked to do it again is a form of passive-aggressive communication.

Again, this form of communication may "work well" in the short term, but it usually leads to poor results. People around us will get frustrated. People who use passive-aggressive communication as their usual mode of conduct know they aren't being sincere, which may ultimately lead to them developing chronic guilt.

OUTCOME: I lose, you lose.

Assertive Communication

The final communication style is assertive communication. This style of communication is rooted in confidence and self-assuredness. This is the type of communicator we want to be. This form of communication means we can respectfully and clearly ask for what we want, and we aren't afraid to say no. People who communicate in this way have confident body language and maintain eye contact; they're relaxed but engaged. They're emphatic but maintain a normal volume and tone of voice. They're secure in their stance—both literally and figuratively—and are unafraid of rejection or disagreement from the recipient.

If somebody says, "Do you want to get burgers tonight?" and that's not what you want, you respond with, "Actually, I'm bored with burgers. How about we get some pizza?"

If you're having trouble with somebody at work, you can go to your boss and say, "Hey, I'm having some issues working with Meg on our current project. I think it would be helpful if the objectives and roles were more clearly defined for this project." This is communicating assertively in a way that will benefit not only you but also Meg and the entire project.

Many people tend to confuse the directness of assertive communication for aggressiveness. This is typically due to the fact that we were trained at an early age to be obedient or overly accommodating to others. Some people hear the word assertiveness, and they envision this as being rude or pushy. This is because they've never had experience with the middle ground between aggressive and passive.

In nearly every situation, assertiveness is the effective way to communicate because you honestly express how you feel while respecting others. You're able to remain level-headed in disagreements and aren't forceful in any way.

OUTCOME: I win, you win.

As you can see, each of these styles results in a different outcome and, with each outcome, there are specific feelings and takeaways for each person involved. From this, you can see why the assertive communication style is the best choice and why, in this book, we emphasize using it in almost every scenario and encounter you find yourself in.

We may use each of these communication styles in different situations, but typically we use only one style the majority of the time. Understanding this about ourselves will aid us in communicating our thoughts and ideas more effectively and help us be better able to receive and understand the communication of others' feelings and ideas. Being honest with ourselves and recognizing which style we use the most can help us to analyze our interactions and see why people may react to us in one way or another. Awareness is the key to changing anything, and choosing the most effective communication style will allow you to gain insight into other people's true personality instead of simply witnessing their reaction to your choice of communication style.

To identify your communication style, examine your body language, your tone of voice, and your choice of words. It's also essential to examine how all of these work together as a whole. By doing this, you'll be able to determine your communication style and then decide whether it's effective or if you should work on changing it.

Misconceptions About Passive-Aggressive Behaviors

Some people have termed passive-aggressive behavior as compliant defiance, sugar-coated hostility, or hostile cooperation. Passive aggression is an oxymoron. This type of behavior doesn't alternate between aggressive and passive behaviors. It combines them into one behavior that irritates and confuses other people.

Passive-aggressive behaviors exist worldwide and can be found at every socio-economic level. This communication style is a masked but deliberate way to express covert anger. Passive aggression involves various behaviors that are designed to get back at others without them being aware of the underlying anger. If used for a long time, passive aggression can be extremely destructive. If you're in a relationship with someone who's passive-aggressive, their communication is usually dysfunctional, discouraging, and confusing.

This kind of behavior is often motivated by a fear of expressing anger. A passive-aggressive person thinks their life will only get worse if others know of their anger, so they find ways to express it indirectly.

Here are some common behaviors that passive-aggressive people use:

• Verbally denying their anger. If you ask them if they're angry, they always deny it. Since they don't feel comfortable with conflict or anger, they deny those emotions, but their outward behaviors will always betray the anger they hold inside.

• Sulking and withdrawing. Because admitting they're angry is too uncomfortable for them, passive-aggressive people show their real emotions by using the silent treatment, sulking, and withdrawing. They might be described as quietly manipulative or brooding because of how they control a person's emotions without saying a word. Sometimes, they cause others to blow up. Even though a passive-aggressive person won't tell you how they're truly feeling, they very much want you to know. Their goal is to make others feel what they feel and have other people act out their anger.

A passive-aggressive person will use technology to stay away from communicating directly since they love avoiding confrontations. They'll use any form of communication other than face-to-face. Vague posts on social media, evasive texts, hostile emails, and an always full voicemail are ways they manage to avoid talking to others.

Chapter 2: People-Pleasing

"The way you treat yourself sets the standard for others." — Sonya Friedman

People-pleasing might not sound all that bad. After all, what's wrong with being nice to people and trying to help them out or make them happy? People pleasers are known for doing whatever it takes to make others happy. While being kind and helpful is generally a good thing, going too far to please others can leave you feeling emotionally depleted, stressed, and anxious. People-pleasers go out of their way to make people like them, even if this uses up their valuable resources or time. They usually act from a lack of self-esteem or insecurity. People-pleasing involves putting someone else's needs ahead of your own. By prioritizing the happiness of others, people-pleasers sacrifice and do whatever it takes to keep other people happy.

Many people-pleasers confuse people-pleasing with kindness, thinking they "don't want to be selfish" and "want to be a good person." People-pleasers tend to struggle with anxiety and themes of control and perfectionism. They want to keep everyone satisfied, but they often sacrifice their needs and desires in the process.

People-pleasing ultimately is a coping mechanism in which your concern about what others think of you has a negative impact on you as you seek external validation and acceptance. Below are some signs that might point to you being a people-pleaser:

1. You always say yes to going to a function that you don't want to attend.
2. You usually apologize for the smallest of perceived slights or errors.

3. You might feel anxious if someone gets mad at you.

4. You automatically laugh when someone else laughs, even if you don't think the source of their laughter is funny.

5. You offer to help others even if you're extremely busy.

6. You act interested even if something bores you.

7. You go against your values to please others and regret it later.

8. You always feel responsible for other people's emotions.

9. You never give your own opinion. You go with whatever other people want.

10. You never say no.

Does any of the above sound like you? If you realize that you've always been a people-pleaser and want to change, there's hope.

Signs That You're a People-Pleaser

Thinking about others and wanting them to be happy

is a good thing, but trying to please others can result in altering or editing your behavior and words to accommodate other people's reactions and feelings.

You may go out of your way to make the people around you happy based on what you assume they need or want. You constantly expend your energy and time just to make them like you. This will be problematic for you in the long run. If you try to please everyone else and always believe that others' needs and wants are more important than your own, this negatively effects you and your relationships.

If you still aren't sure if you're a people-pleaser or are just being exceedingly nice to other people, here are some signs that point to you being a people-pleaser:

- Your Opinion of Yourself Is Low

Most people who try to always please others have low self-esteem, and they get their self-worth from other people's approval. They might think things like, "I'm only worthy of love if I give everything to others."

You might think that others only care for you when

you're being useful, and you need their appreciation and praise just to feel good about yourself.

- You Crave Validation

You have this intrinsic need for others to like you. Whether it's people you're close with or absolute strangers, you can't tolerate it when someone has a negative opinion about you. To avoid this, you'll do anything to please them.

If you're a people-pleaser, you're highly concerned about being rejected. Worrying about this typically leads to certain actions designed to keep others happy so they won't reject you. You could also have a strong desire to feel needed, thinking that you have a better chance of gaining affection from those who need you.

- You Just Can't Say No

You may worry that telling someone "no" or not helping them will make them think you don't care. Always doing what they want seems like a better option, even if you don't have the inclination or time to help. Most people-pleasers agree to do things they don't want to do, such as helping a friend move.

43

Patterns like this can cause problems because they indicate to others that what they need is more important to you than your feelings or comfort. Some people will abuse this. They ignore your boundaries since they know you're going to do it anyway.

- You Accept The Blame Even If You Aren't At Fault

Do you always say "I'm sorry" when something goes wrong? When you're a people-pleaser, you're ready to take on the blame even if the thing that happened wasn't your fault.

Let's say your boss asked you to order pizza for lunch, but the restaurant got the order wrong. They forgot the gluten-free pizzas that you ordered, so some coworkers didn't get to eat. The receipt plainly showed "gluten-free," so it was clearly the restaurant's mistake, but you still apologize over and over. You feel terrible and think that your coworkers have lost faith in you and won't ever trust you again to order lunch.

- You Agree Quickly, Even Though You Don't

Being agreeable sometimes feels like a good way to get

approval. Let's say your coworkers proposed their ideas for a new project during a morning meeting. You might tell one coworker, "What a wonderful idea!" and you tell another, "That's a fantastic plan." Their ideas for the project are totally different, and deep down, you may not agree with either one of them. If you go along with things you don't agree with just to keep the peace, you're setting yourself up for more and more frustration. If both coworkers' plans have flaws, you're doing everybody a disservice when you don't speak up and tell them.

- You Have Problems Being Authentic

Being a people-pleaser can cause you to have a hard time seeing the way people truly are. Constantly pushing your needs away will make it harder to see them clearly, and, eventually, you may not be sure about what you need or want or even how to be true to yourself.

You might not be able to voice your feelings, even though you want to. Here's an example: You may avoid telling your significant other that they did something to make you feel bad. You might think: "They didn't mean it, so if I say something, I'll just hurt their feelings." You deny the fact that they hurt your feelings.

- You Give Too Much

Do you love giving to other people? Do you do this with a goal in mind of them liking you more? Most people-pleasers tend to give so much that they make too many sacrifices. When you make sacrifices, it feeds your sense of self, but it could also create a sense of martyrdom. You may give and keep giving with the hope that people will do the same for you.

- No Free Time

Just being busy doesn't mean you're a people-pleaser, but you need to look hard at how you spend your free time. What do you have left after you take care of your responsibilities like childcare, household chores, and work? Is there time for relaxing or hobbies?

Try to think back to the last time you actually did something for yourself. Can you think of more than one moment like that? If you can't, you might just be a people-pleaser.

- Conflicts and Arguments Upset You

People focused on pleasing others tend to fear anger. This seems pretty logical. When you're angry, it means "I'm not happy." If your main goal is to keep others happy, and they get angry, it means you haven't pleased them. In order to stay away from anger, you may rush to apologize or do things that you think will make them happy even if they aren't angry.

You may be afraid of conflict that doesn't have anything to do with you. If you see two friends arguing, you may try to give them some advice on how to fix the situation so they'll make up. You might even secretly hope they'll think well of you for helping them.

Ways It Can Affect You

Of course, wanting to please others isn't completely negative. When you're in a relationship, pleasing the other person means you have to take their feelings, needs, and wants into account. These types of tendencies usually come from a place of affection and concern.

However, trying to please others and neglecting your own feelings and needs could ultimately hurt you and your relationships.

Here are some repercussions of trying to please others:

- You Feel Resentful and Frustrated

If you're constantly doing for others, the ones you're helping may appreciate and see these sacrifices—but then again, they may not. Over time, they may begin taking advantage of you, even if this isn't their intention. They might not even know you've been making sacrifices for them.

Whatever the case might be, being nice but having ulterior motives can cause you to feel resentment and frustration. This can bubble over into passive-aggressive behaviors that could upset or confuse others who don't know what's happening.

- Others Take Advantage

Some people may recognize and take advantage of your people-pleasing efforts. They might not be able to put a name on their behavior, but knowing that you'll do whatever they ask, they just keep on asking. You'll continue to say yes because you want them to be happy.

This could have some severe consequences. You may encounter serious financial problems if you have family and friends who always ask for money. You might be at a higher risk for emotional or mental abuse along with being manipulated.

If you have children, being a people-pleaser could have other consequences. You may allow your child to not do their chores because you want them to love you. This keeps them from learning the valuable life skills that they need. They may be happy right now, but soon, they'll have some hard lessons to learn about responsibility.

- Relationships Aren't Satisfying

Strong and healthy relationships are balanced and include "give and take" by those involved. You do things for the ones you love, and they should do the same in return. You aren't going to have fulfilling relationships when the people in your life only like you because you do things for them.

Genuinely caring for others isn't a commodity. If you think of yourself as a person who's always giving, but you feel resentful and not valued, you don't have an authentic relationship with yourself. It's hard to maintain satisfying relationships if you aren't truly present to yourself.

- Burned Out And Stressed

The biggest impact of people-pleasing is you're constantly stressed. This can happen when you take on more than you're able to handle. You aren't just losing out on the time you need for yourself, but you don't even have the time to do what you need to do. To get what you must do accomplished, you have to work long into the night, and often you don't get enough sleep. This will inevitably cause physical consequences as well as mental afflictions such as stress and worry.

- People Around You Get Frustrated

Your significant other may notice how you always agree with everybody and wonder why you're always apologizing for something you didn't do. It's easy to get into the habit of always helping others who aren't close to you but not putting any energy and time into your intimate relationships.

In addition, being a people-pleaser could backfire if you're constantly doing for others to the point that you take away their ability to do anything for themselves. The people around you might get mad if you don't tell the truth or you start changing the facts about what happened just to spare their feelings.

- You Have Trust Issues

If you're a people-pleaser, you often aren't always honest with others, and your actions are only meant to satisfy your people-pleasing needs. When you're aware that you're capable of lying convincingly, it won't be long until you start mistrusting others. There will always be doubt in your mind regarding their authenticity.

Where It Comes From

Individuals become people-pleasers for several reasons. There isn't just one cause for these tendencies. They usually develop from several factors, including the following:

- Trauma in Your Past

People-pleasing behaviors sometimes arise due to a fear response associated with some type of trauma. If you've ever experienced trauma like child abuse or domestic violence, you might not feel safe creating boundaries. You might have figured out that it was just safer to do what others wanted of you and deny your own needs. You may have found that constantly pleasing others made you feel safe and likable.

- Problems with Self-Esteem

Sometimes people engage in people-pleasing behavior because they don't value their own desires and needs. Due to a lack of self-confidence, people-pleasers need external validation, and they may feel that doing things for others will lead to that approval and acceptance.

- Fear of Being Rejected

A person might develop a people-pleasing attitude if they have an inherent fear of being rejected. This fear arises from an underlying lack of self-confidence. They try to please others because they worry that people won't like them if they don't go above and beyond to make them happy.

- Symptom of a Mental Health Condition

This behavior can be a symptom of a mental health condition like anxiety, depression, avoidant personality disorder, borderline personality disorder (BPD), or dependent personality disorder.

Ways You Can Stop

If you'd like to break the pattern of pleasing others at your own expense, you must be able to see these behaviors when they show up. By increasing your awareness of how you people-please, you can begin to make some changes. Here are some ways to do that:

- If You Mean It, Show Some Kindness

It's okay to practice kindness. What you need to understand is that kindness doesn't come from wanting to earn someone's approval. It usually doesn't involve any other motive beyond wanting to make someone's life easier.

However, before you offer to help, think about your intentions and how they make you feel. Will this opportunity to be of assistance bring you joy? Will you feel resentful if the person you're helping doesn't return the favor?

- Put Yourself First

You need emotional resources and energy if you want to help other people. If you don't take the time to take care of yourself, you won't be able to do anything for anybody. When you put yourself first, you aren't being selfish; you're taking care of yourself so you'll be able to help others.

It's okay to be a caring, giving person, but it's equally important to tend to and honor your own needs. These needs might include giving your opinion in a meeting, being comfortable with your feelings and emotions, and asking for what you need in a relationship.

- Set Boundaries

Creating healthy boundaries is essential to overcoming your people-pleasing behaviors. When somebody asks you for help, or if you're tempted to intervene in a situation, think about:

1. The way you feel about it. Is this what you truly want to do, or does just thinking about it fill you with dread?
2. Will you have the time to take care of yourself? Are you going to have to sacrifice valuable time or not do a chore that needs to be done?
3. How does helping others make you feel? Does it make you feel resentful or happy?

- Stop Volunteering

Whatever the problem might be, you're always ready to provide someone with a solution. You constantly volunteer for tasks at work, or you give suggestions if a friend or acquaintance mentions they have a problem.

The next time this happens, try to challenge yourself and not offer to assist until somebody asks for your help. If your significant other starts going off about their awful boss, show them you care by listening rather than giving them tips about handling the problem. They likely want validation or empathy more than anything else.

- Find A Therapist

It isn't easy to break patterns you've had for several years, and it's even more challenging to overcome those created in childhood or from trauma. Talking to a therapist could help you discover your compulsion to always try to keep others happy. Even if there isn't a clear cause, they could give you some guidance or coping strategies to help you identify the specific ways in which you try to please others.

Pleasing others at your expense doesn't help anyone. If you're constantly feeling frustrated and unfulfilled because you're trying to keep everybody happy, consider talking to a therapist about effective methods to overcome your people-pleasing behaviors and find real happiness.

CHAPTER 3: WHAT DOES IT MEAN TO BE ASSERTIVE?

"To be passive is to let others decide for you. To be aggressive is to decide for others. To be assertive is to decide for yourself. And to trust that there is enough, that you are enough." — Edith Eva Eger

Assertiveness is a skill that can help a person to better manage situations, themselves, and people. It serves as a way to influence others to gain agreement, acceptance, or behavior change. The assertive person is in control of themselves, and they're fully honest with others and themselves.

Assertiveness is all about balance. It means that you're open about what you need and want while also considering the wants, needs, and rights of others. To be assertive means that you're self-assured, which allows you to firmly and fairly get your point across.

It can be challenging to identify assertive behaviors if we're unclear about the difference between aggression and assertiveness. For this reason, we'll explore these two behaviors in detail to help differentiate them.

Aggressive behavior is all about winning. An aggressive person is only looking out for their best interests and doesn't care about the desires, feelings, needs, or rights of others. When you act aggressively, the power behind it is entirely selfish. You often come across as a bully or pushy. You take everything you want without asking.

Let's say your boss gives you a huge pile of work to do the afternoon before you're scheduled to leave on vacation, and he demands that it be done right now. This is an act of aggression. The work may need to be done immediately, but by giving it all to you at an

58

inappropriate time, the boss isn't thinking about your feelings and needs.

Your assertive response to your boss is that you'll do the work when you return from your vacation. You find that sweet spot between aggression (becoming hostile toward him) and passivity (just doing the work without saying anything). You assert your rights while recognizing that your boss still needs the work done.

While communication is the most common way of displaying assertiveness, there's much more to assertiveness than communication. It all comes down to your values. It means that you're living your life according to what you want and value and not the desires of others.

Assertiveness keeps you from second-guessing the decisions you make. When you make a decision and then spend time second-guessing it, you're telling your brain that you can't trust the decisions you make. However, when you stop second-guessing and worrying about your decisions, you recognize that you feel confident in yourself and your beliefs.

Assertiveness also means that you're careful when you set goals for yourself. When you set reasonable goals, think about how to achieve them, and continue to work toward them, you reinforce the idea that you're reliable and competent.

Assertiveness Isn't a Personality Trait, It's a Skill

It's common for people to say, "I can't be assertive. It's just not who I am." You need to understand that assertiveness isn't a personality trait. It isn't something that you're born with. While some people seem to be naturally more assertive than others, assertiveness isn't a fixed characteristic. Assertiveness is a skill that anyone can learn, and like any other skill, it will take time to learn and develop.

Benefits of Assertiveness

Being assertive allows you to communicate your needs and wants more authoritatively while also being empathetic and fair to others. It can improve your self-confidence, and it can go a long way to improving your overall mental health. Assertiveness also gives you other benefits that can help you in all areas of your life. These benefits include:

- Experiencing more job satisfaction – You'll feel confident in saying yes or no to tasks, and you'll maintain healthy boundaries.
- Decreasing social anxiety – As you become more skilled at expressing your needs, beliefs, and wants, you'll feel less concerned about the disapproval of others.
- Feeling less stressed and anxious – You'll be more self-assured and won't feel as victimized or threatened when things go differently than you expected.
- Having more self-respect and self-confidence – Every time you choose to avoid expressing what you want, you're telling your brain that your wishes aren't important. If you do this repeatedly and consistently, you train yourself to believe you aren't important at all.
- Becoming a more effective problem-solver – You'll feel empowered to do whatever you need to do to help you find the best solution.

- Feeling less resentful of others – When you don't communicate assertively, you often project your disappointments onto others.
- Negotiating win-win solutions – You can spot the value in your opponent's position and find common ground.
- Improving partnerships and relationships – In nearly every relationship issue, communication is the problem, and all communication problems come down to issues with assertiveness.
- Becoming a great manager – You know how to get things done while treating others with respect and fairness, which means you'll be treated the same way in return.

Why Is Being Assertive Important?

- You'll become more self-assured – Assertiveness teaches you to be assured of your wants and desires and, therefore, more confident about yourself. You start discovering the reasons behind your actions and find the incentive to follow your dreams.

- It increases your creativity – When you have fewer things to worry about, you have more time to try out new things and excel creatively. Stress doesn't allow you to do that. In the absence of stress, it's easier for ideas to arise and for you to feel confident to venture out creatively.

- It teaches you to not settle for less – When you appreciate your own efforts, you start realizing how precious you are. You start giving all your efforts their deserved value, which makes you aim higher. This helps you to not settle for less and not compromise in situations where you shouldn't. In this way, assertiveness adds value to your life.

Barriers to Assertiveness

We'll now explore some of the most common obstacles people face when trying to be assertive. If any of these obstacles are familiar to you, that's the first step in understanding how to combat them. Let's take a look at some of these:

1.   Wanting everybody to recognize you

If being nice to everyone is always your number-one priority, you've diminished your freedom to maneuver. Searching for recognition is a legitimate and natural need. However, when you're too sensitive about what others think of you, it can cause you to stop acting in your own best interest, and you could lose your independence.

2.   Wanting to be loved at any cost

All humans want is to be loved and to have affection. However, wanting to be appreciated and loved at all costs can lead to dependence on others. Demanding the respect of others while being respectful can help your self-esteem grow.

3.   Seeking to control all situations

This is sometimes called the "superman complex." It's best to avoid thinking of yourself as the "savior." It's far better if you choose to participate in a more collective manner.

4.   Wanting to impose your ideas on others at all costs

You have to give others the chance to disagree and allow them to exercise their freedom of speech and thought. Trying to impose your ideas on others isn't an effective means to properly manage conflicts.

5. Trying to get sympathy by overworking

You have to respect your own limits, and overworking yourself to get the sympathy of others isn't the way to do that.

6. Wanting to be perfect in everything you do

To counter the tendency to feel you need to be perfect, start focusing on the essential parts of things and look to ensure you add value in the longer run.

7. Setting conflicting goals for yourself

Taking on responsibilities while also trying to avoid all conflicts will prove to be a major disappointment. Moreover, to reach relevant and realistic goals, you have to set a defined target. If you can't state specifically what your goal is, how to reach it, and the time you need to reach it, you're setting yourself up for failure.

8. Not allowing yourself to fail

If you constantly tell yourself that you "can't do anything wrong," you forget that failing is a normal part of life. Fear of failure puts unnecessary stress on yourself.

One commonality in all of these points that get in our way of being assertive is fear: We act passively to avoid upsetting other people or avoid drama. We act aggressively so we can feel powerful and alleviate our deep-seated insecurities.

When we use one of the three ineffective communication styles, it may help to avoid negative feelings or conflict in the short term. However, in the long term, this usually has an adverse effect. If we behave passively, we end up feeling chronically dissatisfied. If we behave aggressively, we end up being socially isolated and lonely. If we exhibit passive-aggressive behavior, we lose the respect and trust of others.

CHAPTER 4: HOW ASSERTIVE ARE YOU?

"No one can make you feel inferior without your consent." – Eleanor Roosevelt

You've been planning on having dinner with your friend. On the morning of the dinner, the person you've had a crush on asks you out. So, do you say yes to the person and disappoint your friend?

You finally got that raise you were promised a year ago. Do you put it into your retirement fund or take the vacation of your dreams?

You've been trying to get a head start on a report you need to turn in today, but your neighbor's pet is sick and needs your assistance; what do you make a priority—your neighbor or your work?

In life, we're faced with countless decisions, both small and big, that create hard choices. Even though several factors are involved, our core values are the main thing that guides us. Our values dictate the type of person we are or want to be and guide our actions.

How can we know what these core values are? This section will show you how you can discover or choose these values.

What are core values? Core values are a set of fundamental beliefs, ideals, or practices that inform how you conduct your life, both personally and professionally. Core values are qualities that represent an individual's highest priorities, deeply held beliefs, and core, fundamental driving forces. They allow us to make important decisions, grow, and handle any adversity we might face.

When looking at your path toward personal development, you have to keep your core values in mind to help you achieve your goals. Without reflecting upon your values, you'll simply react to circumstances by making careless decisions that will hold you back in the long run. When you're aware of your core values, the road to success will be much easier because you'll innately know what factors in your life you want to focus on in order to feel fulfilled. Your goals will be clear because you'll recognize your passions and what makes you happy, and you'll align your actions with your skills to ultimately be successful.

You might have learned most of your values from your caregivers, society, religious leaders, teachers, and parents. You've probably rebelled against most of these values from time to time or even changed your mind about some of them as you learned more about yourself and the world around you. There are ways to discover which core values mean the most to you.

Choosing Your Core Values

If you aren't sure what your core values are or want to clarify which ones are at the top of your list, here are some ways to help do that. Pick eight values from the list below. You'll see "other" at the bottom of the list, so make good use of this.

1. Freedom
2. Serenity
3. Success
4. Work
5. Family
6. Adventure
7. Security
8. Self-preservation
9. Survival
10. Leadership
11. Learning
12. Relationship
13. Connection
14. Love
15. Gratitude
16. Bravery

17. Beauty

18. Loyalty

19. Dependability

20. Creativity

21. Accomplishment

22. Nature

23. Fitness

24. Health

25. Compassion

26. Financial security

27. Other

Now look at your top eight values. You can change your mind about these any time you want to. It's perfectly natural to change the values that are most important to you as you face a challenging or new situation. Some values might represent enduring ideals that you'd only change if you were under duress. Keep in mind that your choice might not involve a decision between wrong and right but between two cherished values.

Think about the six people you admire the most and why they mean so much to you. Your core values could be personified in the people you admire. You can use a simple process to find the values that you associate with these people.

First, identify and write down the people you consider to be your role models. Now think about the values they represent. Your list could include your father for his kindness and gentleness, your wife for her love and acceptance, or your coworker for their listening skills.

Look at yourself. Each day of your life, think about the choices you make. Do this for several days and try your best to consciously place a label on the values that help you make decisions at home and at work. Pay attention to whether you embody and display the values you chose. If you don't, which values do you express or live by? Do you see any patterns? Is there anything you can learn from the things you want, the things you would be willing to give up, and the things that aren't negotiable? If you experience any dissatisfaction with any of your choices, you might not be living your core values.

The Way Other People See You

Have you ever met someone and knew immediately that you didn't like them? Even though growing up, we were told not to make any snap judgments about others, we constantly do it, and most of these are accurate.

Humans are social creatures, and our ancestors evolved intuition that helps us process all kinds of social information. This intuition takes in all kinds of data points, assesses them, and then generates feelings or ideas about who we've just met. We might decide they're attractive, trustworthy, friendly, or likable, or maybe we don't believe they're any of these. Processing this information doesn't take place inside our awareness. All we're conscious of is the feeling that results deep in your gut that creates a judgment about this person.

It isn't clear which social cues our intuition uses to make these judgments, but it's been posited that they're based on reading subtle vocal inflections, facial expressions, and body posture.

A person's personality comprises their unique characteristics. How are you different from your sister, brother, next-door neighbor, etc.? We don't always look at a person in terms of personality traits, but we evaluate them by how they're different from us and other people we know. Obtaining accurate personality profiles is hard to do because of cognitive biases.

It shouldn't surprise you that people who've known you for a long time know your personality better than someone you just met. But it often happens that the people who know us best and like us for who we are overlook or forgive behaviors that aren't healthy for us—or our relationships. Find someone who knows you well and with whom you have difficulties, and try to talk to them about the issues between you. If you communicate with them assertively, you could resolve the problem and make a new friend.

Self-Image and the Way You See Yourself

Self-image is both a subconscious and conscious way of looking at yourself. This is the emotional judgment we've made about our self-worth. We create self-images by interacting with others while taking into account the way they react to us and how they categorize us. Their worldview influences the way they respond to us, and this can also prevent them from having an accurate picture of themselves.

Humans naturally compare themselves to others even though they try not to. People typically assess themselves based on the expectations of their family and friends. Most of the time, society gives us a particular role, such as being a good parent or having a good career. This can contribute to the way we look at ourselves.

We're constantly assessing ourselves. If we have a positive self-image, this can lead to self-acceptance and confidence. If we have a negative self-image, this can lead to depression or feeling inferior. People who develop a realistic and mature self-image won't come unglued with each critical comment they receive.

When you have low self-esteem, you tend to see yourself, the world, and your future more negatively and critically. You might feel anxious, sad, low, or unmotivated. When you encounter challenges, you may doubt your ability to overcome them. You might talk to yourself harshly in your mind, telling yourself things like "You're stupid," "You'll never manage this," or, "I don't amount to anything."

The negative beliefs and opinions you hold about yourself are at the center of low self-esteem. Nobody is born with beliefs like this—they develop as a result of the experiences you have throughout your life. How other people treat you—particularly when you're growing up—can significantly affect how you see yourself.

The good news is that it's entirely possible to overcome low self-esteem! There are two key components to combatting this negative self-image. The first is to stop listening to your critical inner voice. The second is to start practicing self-compassion.

Research into self-esteem shows that both low and high self-esteem can create emotional and social problems for individuals. While high levels of self-esteem can be linked to narcissism and aggressive behaviors, low levels of self-esteem may cause social anxiety, passiveness, and depression. The healthiest type of self-esteem is moderate self-esteem based on valuing one's inherent worth as a person and rather than comparing oneself to others. In this sense, if your goal is to develop more self-confidence, it's better to focus on having high levels of self-worth rather than high levels of self-esteem.

Self-worth usually comes up in therapy. An individual can boost their self-worth through acceptance and understanding. You can help yourself by monitoring your internal dialogue, acknowledging your accomplishments, being tolerant and assertive, and spending time with friends. Self-worth can be improved by valuing your talents and skills, respecting your intelligence, and acting on your feelings and beliefs. Keeping a healthy balance involves being able to focus your attention on others.

Assertiveness Quiz

In this section, you'll be able to determine your current level of assertiveness so you can assess where you are now compared to where you want to be in the future. Here's a quick quiz for you to take.

1. You go to your favorite fast-food restaurant and order a chicken sandwich with mayonnaise, but when you receive your sandwich, it doesn't have any mayo on it. Would you:
   a. Accept it
   b. Angrily refuse the sandwich and yell at the cashier until they summon their manager
   c. Let them know of the mistake in a polite manner and ask them to fix it

2. You're waiting in line to be served. Suddenly, somebody cuts in front of you. Would you:
   a. Let them stay
   b. Pull them out of line and yell at them to go to the end of the line
   c. Tell the person that you're waiting in line and point out where the end of the line is

3. After you leave the store, you notice that you were short-changed. Would you:

    a. Let it go since you've already left and the cashier is busy with somebody else

    b. Go to the manager, yell about what happened, and demand the problem be fixed

    c. Go back to the cashier and let them know what happened in a respectful manner

4. You're watching a TV show you really like when somebody asks you to help them with something. Would you:

    a. Do what they ask as quickly as you can

    b. Say "no" and continue watching the show

    c. Ask if it can wait until after your show is over, and then go do it

5. A friend drops by, but they hang out for too long, keeping you from working on something important. Would you:

    a. Let them stay and try to squeeze in as much work as possible later on

    b. Tell them to leave and stop bothering you

    c. Explain to them that you have something to work on and ask if they can come by later

6. You ask for a small drink, but you're given a large one by mistake. Would you:

    a. Pay for the bigger drink since they already poured it

    b. Demand to speak with the manager and make a big deal out of it

    c. Remind them that you ordered a small drink and request that they give you what you originally ordered

7. You think that somebody has a grudge against you, but you're not sure why. Would you:

    a. Pretend you don't know anything about it

    b. Get even with them

    c. Ask them why they may be mad at you to gain an understanding

8. You take a gaming console in for repairs, and you get a written estimate. When you pick it up, you're billed for an amount a lot higher than the estimate. Would you:

    a. Pay it

    b. Refuse to pay, complain about the excess price, and demand to speak with a higher-up

    c. Indicate that you agreed to the estimated amount and pay only that price

9. You invite a friend over to your house for a party, but they never show up, nor do they call you to let you know why. Would you:

    a. Ignore it but also not show up at something they invite you to

    b. Call them names and complain to your other friends about them

    c. Call them to find out what happened

10. You're discussing a group project that includes your teacher. One of the other students asks you about an aspect of the project, but you don't know how to respond. Would you:

    a. Make up an answer that's plausible so your teacher thinks you're on top of it

    b. Don't answer, but attack the other student for their stupid question

    c.   Mention that you aren't sure, but offer to provide them with more information later

Count up how many a's, b's, and c's you have.

If you have mostly "a" choices, you have a more passive communication style. If you have six or more "a" choices, you're probably mostly passive in your interpersonal actions.

If you have more "b" choices, you have a more aggressive style. Six or more "b" choices means you exhibit aggressive interpersonal behavior.

If you have more "c" choices, you have a more assertive style. Six or more "c" choices means you have an assertive interpersonal behavior.

In addition to this quiz, you can determine your level of assertiveness by taking the free assertiveness quiz at: www.howassertiveareyou.com.

CHAPTER 5: SELF-AWARENESS

"Don't wait until everything is just right. It will never be perfect. There will always be challenges, obstacles and less than perfect conditions. So what? Get started now. With each step you take, you will grow stronger and stronger, more and more skilled, more and more self-confident, and more and more successful." -- Mark Victor Hansen

Before we dive into the techniques that can help you become more assertive, it's essential that you learn how to shift your mindset to be more self-aware. The way you view yourself is central to how you relate with others.

83

Let's take ourselves back in time to 1100 CE. We're sitting on a wooden bench, holding a quill, and writing out a list of traits that we believe to be good in a family member, colleague, lover, or friend. What might some of those traits be that we put down on this old-timey list? It may be things like patience, generosity, loyalty, and kindness. Now, come back to the present day. Even though we're sitting in a modern living room and writing out a similar list on our computer or phone, there's a good chance we'll jot down the same virtues that we did back in 1100, but some newer concepts might get added. In fact, I'd add self-awareness as a good trait in a person. But what does self-awareness mean?

Self-awareness has to do with recognizing and managing emotions. This term goes back to Carl Jung and Sigmund Freud. Still, our understanding of self-awareness today is likely derived from Daniel Goleman's book *Emotional Intelligence*, published in 1995. Simply put, self-awareness is how well a person recognizes their own emotional state at any given time. The issue here is that most of us are unaware of our emotional state. We also don't realize how much our emotional state influences our thoughts and actions. The more we can manage our emotional states, the better we'll manage all aspects of our lives.

Self-awareness also allows you to come out of yourself and see how your actions and words affect others. It's a type of introspection that doesn't shut out the world but brings the world in for an assessment correlated with how you feel and act.

Most of us believe we're self-aware when, in fact, we aren't. People tend to overestimate how self-aware they are. They feel they know themselves well, but the truth is, they don't. They might have even steered clear of cultivating self-awareness because it meant looking at themselves honestly, which can create a lot of tough feelings to have to contend with.

In any case, genuine self-awareness is invaluable. It used to be that lacking self-awareness was brushed off as a benign human quirk, but as our world changes, this need for self-awareness has become of greater importance. If you know how to manage your emotions, you'll have a better chance of influencing the emotions of people in your family, in a social situation, or at work.

Build Self-Confidence

When you have self-confidence, you trust in your own abilities and judgments. You feel worthy and value yourself no matter what imperfections you might have or what other people might think about you.

Self-esteem and self-efficacy are used interchangeably with self-confidence, but they're a bit different. We feel a sense of self-efficacy when we notice we've achieved a goal or mastered a skill. This helps us believe that we'll succeed if we work hard and learn more in a particular area. This kind of confidence enables you to accept hard challenges and persevere when you face setbacks.

Self-esteem means you believe the people around you like and approve of you. You might or might not have the ability to control these feelings, and if you experience rejection or criticism from others, your self-esteem could suffer if you don't find ways to support it.

Confidence is a big player when it comes to being assertive. If you aren't confident, you'll be less likely to speak up for yourself. You simply don't believe you deserve to have your needs known or ideas expressed.

Let's take a look at how to know if you're confident. The following examples show the difference between actions considered a display of confidence and actions that demonstrate low self-confidence.

1. Confident Actions
    a. Graciously accept compliments: "Thanks, I worked hard on that. I'm glad you can see the effort I put into it."
    b. Expecting to be congratulated on your accomplishments.
    c. Admitting that you made a mistake and learning from it.
    d. Willing to take a risk and go the extra mile to make something better.
    e. Do what you think is right even if you might be criticized or mocked.
2. Low Self-Confidence Actions

a. Dismissing compliments: "That project wasn't anything. Anybody could have done it."
b. Praising other people for your virtues.
c. Trying to cover up the mistakes you make or hoping you can fix them before anybody else notices them.
d. Staying in your comfort zone, avoiding risks, and being afraid to fail.
e. Basing your actions on what others think about you.

Self-confident people tend to be more positive. They value themselves, and they trust their own judgment. The good news is you can learn to be more confident. Here are some ways to project confidence:

Body Language

To make yourself feel and look more confident, you need to adopt an open posture. Stand or sit straight. Keep your hands either folded in your lap or down at your sides. Don't stand with your hands on your hips. This communicates your desire to be dominant. Never slouch!

Keep your head up and level. Don't lean backward or forward. If you're making a presentation, use open hand gestures. When you need to "point" to something, spread your hand and keep the palm facing the audience. This shows you're willing to share ideas and communicate. Make sure your upper arms stay close to your body.

Communicate Face-to-Face

You have to engage with others in all aspects of your life. When you engage with another person, make and keep eye contact while you're talking. This shows them you're interested in what they're saying. It also shows that you're an active participant in the conversation. Keep in mind that the cultural differences in body language are vast. Gestures that mean one thing in your part of the world can mean the exact opposite somewhere else. As a result, it's quite possible to offend someone without even opening your mouth and with no ill will on your part! Do some research if you're making a presentation or interacting with people from different countries.

Never look away from the person or fidget while the conversation is happening. This might make you look anxious or distracted. If you normally shake hands when greeting someone at your job, make sure your handshake is firm. You don't want it to be too firm, and don't go overboard if you don't know the person. If you reach for the other person's shoulder or wrist with your other hand, it might be seen as a show of dominance. Therefore, this isn't recommended when you meet someone for the first time. Don't make the encounter awkward or painful.

Look at Your Accomplishments

You increase your self-confidence when you can say: "I can do this, and here is how I know this to be true." As a part of your analysis, you should have discovered what you're good at.

Create an achievement log and list 10 things you're most proud of. Maybe you scored the highest possible score on your SATs. Maybe you got the highest grade on the final exam. Maybe you beat out the competition in getting the job promotion. Maybe you did something that had a positive impact on somebody's life.

Look at all these achievements and use them to create positive affirmations about your many abilities. Affirmations can be powerful if you have the habit of constantly undermining your confidence by talking negatively about yourself.

Plan Out Your Responses

Do you tend to automatically say yes without thinking about it? If this is the case, you may want to have some go-to phrases at the ready when you're faced with an invitation or request that you don't want to do. Some good ones include:

- "I have a schedule conflict."
- "I need to check my calendar."
- "I won't be able to; I have plans."
- "Let me get back to you on that."

If you go with a reply about checking your schedule, you'll need to get back to the person once you've "checked." It would be rude if you didn't. Just keep in mind that you're never obligated to explain why you turned down an invitation or request.

Besides coming up with statements to say when presented with an invitation or request, you can also practice your assertiveness. Start rehearsing some general scenarios that you may encounter, especially for situations in which you know you'll have a harder time being assertive. Practice your response out loud. You may also find it beneficial to write out a script before practicing. If you have a colleague or friend you trust, you may want to role-play with them. That way, they can provide you with feedback.

When you start practicing your assertiveness skills in real situations, begin with low-risk situations. For example, try being assertive with a friend or partner before moving into bigger, higher-risk situations at work. Each time you're assertive, evaluate yourself to see if you approached the situation in an appropriate manner.

Use Positive Self-Talk

It's really hard to practice assertiveness when you're caught up in the moment. That's why it's a good idea to pump yourself up by using positive self-talk. This might sound corny, but if you're getting ready for a conversation in which you know you're going to have to put your foot down, hyping yourself with the reminders, "My time is important," or, "I've got this," can really help you out.

Self-talk can strongly influence our confidence and ability to be assertive because it can be either positive or negative. Negative self-talk hurts us and causes us to believe we can't do something. It reduces our self-worth, self-confidence, and self-respect—which, of course, affects our ability to be assertive. That negative voice in our head is as bad as a bully demeaning us.

On the other hand, if you have positive self-talk, it makes you more confident and more sure of yourself. Athletes like to use positive, motivational self-talk to help them push through their limits and increase their ability to cope with pain. Try repeating positive

93

affirmations each day and before any difficult conversations you expect to have. You'll be surprised at how affirmations can change your perception of yourself. This shift can be felt in how you view yourself. It can also strengthen your voice and make you feel more self-empowered.

Create a Clear Vision

Having a well-thought-out vision for your life is a critical component for achieving your dreams, aspirations, and what fulfills you. To be assertive, you have to know what it is that you truly want. A critical ingredient for assertiveness is knowing exactly what you're willing to do to achieve your vision as well as knowing what you won't do. Both sides of the coin are equally important in determining how successful you'll be. Clarity helps you eliminate those ideas and activities that don't add value to your vision. A clear vision enables you to draw inward and tap into your resources, skills, and abilities to work with others to propel you forward.

Here are a few simple tips for creating a clear vision for

your life:

1. Be clear about what your vision is. What is it that you're looking to accomplish? Come up with a long-term vision
2. Set clear goals. Come up with shorter-term goals that can help you get to your long-term vision.
3. Practice positive visualization and positive thinking. Think about who you'd like to be and how you want to communicate. Building a positive image of yourself can help reframe how you see yourself, building self-respect and self-confidence.
4. Challenge yourself to change and grow. This is all about stepping outside of your comfort zone and overcoming obstacles and challenges.
5. Focus on the strengths you have. Understand what your strengths are, and use them.

Avoid Guilt

If you can learn how to differentiate between a guilt trip and feeling guilty, you'll be well on your way to becoming more assertive. Many people find themselves feeling guilty whenever they assert themselves. This is generally because they're new to the assertiveness strategy. To say no to a person doesn't mean you're rejecting them.

The important thing to understand is that feeling guilty and being guilt-tripped aren't the same thing. Feeling guilty means you're aware of doing something wrong. The vast majority of passive people have a hard time learning to be assertive because they're afraid of feeling guilty when they don't go along with what others want.

This is a classic trap because it's hard to distinguish fake guilt from real guilt. Picture this: You have a pushy family member who's been giving you a hard time about not hosting Christmas this year. Think about how you'd feel as they describe how nobody else will do it, how it's so important to keep the family together, how everybody depends on you to have the party, and how hurt they're all going to be if you "let them down."

This is what we call a guilt trip. The only reason that pushy family member is saying all those things is to make you feel uncomfortable in the hope you'll feel compelled to host Christmas. The key to this is knowing that the guilt isn't real.

Guilt is an emotion that everyone experiences when we know we've done something bad or wrong. It isn't someone else saying or implying that you've done something wrong. So, whenever you start feeling guilty, ask yourself, "Did I actually do anything wrong?" It takes practice to learn how to tolerate the discomfort you feel because of fake guilt, but you'll be able to do it.

CHAPTER 6: NON-VERBAL STRATEGIES

Non-verbal communication is the act of conveying a thought, feeling, or idea through physical gestures, posture, and facial expressions. Non-verbal communication plays a significant role in our lives as it can improve a person's ability to relate, engage, and establish meaningful interactions.

Each movement and combination of movements of the body—such as shifts in posture, movement of the eyes, gestures, and expressions on the face—provide signals to others. These cues may be subtle or obvious, and they can be contradictory: A person might say one thing while their body language conveys an entirely different message. Because non-verbal communication is often instinctive and typically not easy to fake, it's generally more indicative of a person's true feelings.

Cultural Impact

Before we jump into non-verbal communication and its relationship to assertiveness, it's important to mention that non-verbal communication isn't the same in every culture. Something that's normal or expected in one culture might be seen as offensive in another. As the world has become more accessible, we have the privilege of working with people around the globe. This means you could interact with people from different cultures who have different non-verbal cues.

For example, you're expected to shake hands with people you meet in Western cultures. But that's not the norm in every culture. Shaking hands might have a very different meaning depending on the culture. Before you go into a situation where other cultures may be present, familiarize yourself with what's appropriate and acceptable and what isn't.

Understanding these differences and being mindful of how you communicate non-verbally will make you a better communicator. A big part of this is understanding the cultural impact of non-verbal cues.

Nine Types of Non-Verbal Communication

Non-verbal communication helps you to communicate more effectively and connects you with others. When you understand the various cues, you can learn to tailor your message to prevent miscommunication. When you understand non-verbal cues, you can better understand what other people are telling you. The following are the nine types of non-verbal communication.

1. Body language – This is any non-verbal cue that's communicated by the position of your body. This would include your posture, such as whether you're sitting at attention or slouching. Things like crossing your legs, picking at your nails, crossing your arms, and fidgeting are all a part of body language.

2. Gestures – Body language and gestures are a bit different. Gestures are often more purposeful and tend to be more culturally coded. This can include hand gestures like giving somebody a thumbs up and more subtle gestures like shrugging your shoulders.

3. Facial expressions – Much like gestures, these are often more purposeful. These include things like frowning, nodding, or smiling. However, a lot of our facial expressions tend to be unconscious when we're worried or stressed. For example, your eyes widen when surprised or blink if you hear something loud.

4. Eye contact – This is one of the biggest parts of non-verbal communication. That said, the meaning of eye contact varies greatly among cultures. Many cultures interpret lack of eye contact as disinterest. However, in other cultures, excessive eye contact is considered rude and makes people uncomfortable.

5. Tone of voice – Paralinguistics comprises speaking cadence, speed, value, tone, and voice. For example, you may tend to speak

faster if you're nervous, as many people do. You may also whisper if you're telling a secret.

6. Personal space – Non-verbal cues don't have to do with just body movements. It can also include the way you interact with those around you. The physical distance between you and another person says a lot about your relationship with them. This is another non-verbal cue that varies from culture to culture. The best thing to do is to mirror what the person you're interacting with is doing to avoid making them uncomfortable.

7. Touch – You may not think about touch as a form of communication, but it is. For example, some people make judgments about others based the way they shake hands. Using that same logic, it would probably be inappropriate to high-five your boss, but you may high-five your best friend.

8. Appearance – Clothing plays a big part in how people assess us. Everybody has their unique style, so if a co-worker came into work wearing something they don't typically wear, that could indicate something has changed about them.

9. Personal objects – Much like clothing, objects can provide you with insight into a person. Imagine that one of your co-workers carries around a personal planner all the time. You'd likely assume they're an organized person.

Next, let's look at how we can be assertive in our non-verbal communications.

Non-Verbal Assertiveness Cues

What can you do to improve your assertiveness skills so your body language matches what you say?

Eyes

Eye contact is a significant part of assertiveness. If you look away from the person you're talking with too often, this may telegraph that you're anxious. Firm eye contact—that you break for a second from time to time—helps to make you look confident. If you find holding eye contact difficult, or if you're faced with an intimidating stare, hold your ground by looking at the space between their eyes. This helps to take the sting out of meeting that gaze, and they won't be able to tell that you aren't looking them in the eye.

Voice

Shouting is a big no-no when it comes to assertiveness, as it will cost you your credibility. Whispering is also a bad thing as it shows a lack of confidence. Try to find a middle ground with a well-modulated, calm voice that commands respect and shows that you're self-assured. Try to be mindful of your breathing to lower the physical symptoms of stress. This can also help keep your voice from trembling.

Hands

Your hands can help to add authority to your points. Affirmative hand gestures add more gravitas to your words, and they'll keep you from picking at your clothes, tapping something with your hands, or any other activity that can make you look anxious. If you're sitting at a desk or table during a conversation, interlocking your fingers into a steeple is a clever technique that will keep your hands from messing around nervously.

Posture

You want to make yourself appear authoritative, but you don't want to create an image of looming over your prey when being assertive. That would come off as aggressive. However, you do want to inhabit your space. Notice what you're doing with your body. Use open gestures. If you notice that you've started to make yourself look less assured by wringing your hands or crossing your arms, pause. Open up your gestures so you look confident. When we're nervous, our shoulders tend to travel up to our ears. Relax your shoulders downward as your head remains high.

Feet

Feet are the number-one giveaway of anxiety, so pay attention to them. When sitting, are you shuffling them from side to side, tapping them, or nervously bouncing your leg? Any of these movements lets the other person know you aren't sure of yourself. When standing, ensure your feet are hip-width apart with your knees relaxed, so you have a confident and strong posture. This will keep you from tapping your feet or constantly changing your position. When sitting, you can cross them at the ankles or place them together.

Now you appear self-assured and confident about what you're saying.

Assertive Listening

All of your non-verbal cues come together to let the person you're talking to know you're listening. By listening, you communicate that you're paying attention to what they say. Secondly, you let them know you're trying to understand what they're telling you. It's important to be clear that understanding what a person says differs from agreeing with what they say. A person could be telling you something you'd never agree with, but you can still be an assertive listener to show them you're paying attention.

When someone is talking to you, give them your full attention and ensure that you disregard all distractions. Distractions are the most common disrupter of listening. By doing this, you communicate that they have your undivided attention. It also helps if you lean forward just slightly, as this lets them know you're truly listening. Make sure you have a relaxed posture.

There's an art to assertive listening. Listening in this way means you keep a relaxed state of mind as the other person speaks to you. This gives you the ability to better understand what they're saying so you can ask effective questions to clarify anything you don't understand. Even if you don't say a word, you still communicate with your eyes, facial expressions, gestures, and posture.

Encoding Your Non-Verbal Cues

Encoding meaning into non-verbal cues often seems like a big hurdle, but it's something that happens all the time. While some of our encoded non-verbal cues tend to be accidental, there are movements and gestures that we encode purposefully. Think of foot-tapping, rolling your eyes, or head nods. To encode your non-verbal cues more purposefully, you can give these techniques a try:

1. Be aware of your communication style.

We went over this in a previous chapter, and you took the quiz to see how assertive you are. Being aware of your communication style will help you be more conscious of your assertiveness or lack thereof.

2. Be present in the moment.

Improving your mindfulness is a big part of encoding non-verbal cues. If you're aware of your surroundings and yourself, you'll be in more control of your cues, non-verbal and verbal alike.

3. Work on lowering your stress.

We often unintentionally encode non-verbal cues because of our emotional state. If you're burned out, overworked, or tired, you don't have the mental energy you need to be aware of how you're communicating. Essentially, you remain in a fight-or-flight mode, which will lower your ability to communicate with purpose.

4. Deal with any underlying conditions you may have.

You could encode non-verbal cues without realizing it because of an unconscious or underlying feeling. For example, if you struggle with imposter syndrome—which means you believe you're not as competent as others perceive you to be—you may distance yourself from others without realizing what you're doing. Therefore, before improving your behavior, you need to understand its root cause.

5. Prioritize face-to-face communication if at all possible.

A huge disadvantage to asynchronous communication is that we can't encode non-verbal cues. This causes a greater risk of miscommunication or misunderstanding. When you can, aim for in-person conversations, especially if what you're saying is any form of constructive criticism or if you're talking about something difficult to understand. Face-to-face communication allows the other person to ask questions in real time, which greatly diminishes the possibility of a misunderstanding.

Decoding Cues

The second aspect of non-verbal communication is decoding the non-verbal cues of others. When you accurately decode others' non-verbal cues, this lowers the chances of misunderstanding what they're saying, and it enhances your rapport.

To improve your decoding of the non-verbal cues of others, give these techniques a try:

1. Work on your emotional intelligence.

The first step in decoding any form of communication is to improve your emotional intelligence. Emotional intelligence has to do with recognizing, understanding, and regulating emotions, both yours and others.

2. Develop better listening skills.

Active listening is vital in decoding cues. This means that you listen to understand what another person is saying—not to simply plan out what you're going to say in response. When practicing active listening, you're more present and more engaged, which allows you to pick up on subtle non-verbal cues.

3. Notice discrepancies between what they say and their true feelings.

An important thing about non-verbal communication is that you can pick up on signals that the person may not be verbalizing. For example, if somebody says they're excited about a new project, but they have their arms crossed and look away, they probably aren't as excited as they say. When you notice these cues, you can start to dig for more information. For example, you could try to figure out if they're worried about the project for some reason and then work on a way to reassure them.

4. Improve your cultural intelligence.

Developing your cultural intelligence enhances your ability to read the body language and other cues of people from various cultures. This can help you in business settings, socially, or traveling.

5. If in doubt, just ask.

One of the most significant risks of decoding non-verbal cues is making assumptions that aren't true. You have facts, and you have stories. Facts are the objective truths that anybody can access. Stories are assumptions that you create based on the facts. We all tell ourselves stories, but identifying if these stories are true can prevent a misunderstanding. The best way to do that is to simply ask a question about something you're confused about.

Non-Verbal Traits

Passive

- Nervousness
- Keeps distance
- Hunched shoulders
- Little or no eye contact
- Smiles when criticized
- Frequent throat clearing
- Pauses frequently as if not sure about the appropriateness of the sentence
- Eager to finish the conversation and move on
- Overtly conscious of the implications of the conversation

Aggressive

- Piercing eye contact. Keeps the gaze.
- Eyebrows can be angry (raised) and facial expression is intense
- Body language is defensive/aggressive: arms crossed, legs apart and pointing fingers

- May walk or stride around the place while talking
- Makes loud noises such as banging on the table or makes extra noises by being a bit more forceful when moving objects around

Assertive

- Emotionally relaxed and reserved
- Erect and solid without having a threatening posture
- Good eye contact without seeming to want to demean

A Short Message from the Author

Hi, are you enjoying the book thus far? I'd love to hear your thoughts! Many readers do not know how hard reviews are to come by, and how much they help an author.

I would be incredibly thankful if you could take just 60 seconds to write a brief review, even if it's just a few sentences!

Thank you for taking the time to share your thoughts!

CHAPTER 7: VERBAL STRATEGIES

If we have good verbal communication, this lets others know we're willing and able to interact with them assertively and that we're open and ready to resolve conflicts and address issues calmly and directly. In this section, we're going to look at a few strategies for communicating assertively to ensure you're being heard and respected as well as letting others know you're making your needs a priority.

How To Speak Assertively

Most people think that speaking assertively has to do with being mean. This is incorrect. Assertiveness is about knowing what you want and need and communicating this concisely and clearly while showing consideration and respect for others.

Assertiveness is a communication style that empowers and enables you to voice your needs and opinions without being a people-pleaser or aggressive. This section includes strategies you can use to become more assertive.

- Focus on the Three C's

When speaking assertively, it's essential to keep the Three C's in mind as you deliver your message:

1. Confident – Speak confidently to show you believe in your ability to handle the situation.
2. Clear – Ensure the message is clear and easy to understand.
3. Controlled – Ensure you deliver the message in a calm and controlled manner.

- Use "I" Statements

When you use "I" statements, you take responsibility for what you're feeling rather than blaming someone else. Telling others what you're feeling gives you a solution that won't be confrontational but will allow you to be acknowledged and heard.

Here are some examples:

Rather than saying, "You're so annoying when you interrupt me," say, "When you interrupt me, I feel annoyed."

Don't say, "You don't care." Say, "I feel ignored."

Don't say, "You're wrong." Say, "I don't agree."

Don't say, "You hurt me." Say, "I feel hurt."

- Stay Focused on the Facts

Stay away from accusing others by only focusing on the facts. In this way, you can state how whatever happened affected you. Look at this example: "You've been coming home late for the past week (fact). I'm concerned (how this is affecting you.)." You avoided being confrontational. If you would have said: "You've been coming home late for the past week, and you're really trying my patience. What's going on?" you just made the situation confrontational.

- Acknowledging Other's Emotions

During a heated conversation, if you can acknowledge the other person's emotions and reactions, this shows your goal isn't to get into a debate right then but talk things over at a later time. This can help diffuse the situation while allowing you to begin afresh once things have cooled down. You could say something like, "I sense your frustration. It's understandable in this situation. Perhaps we could continue this conversation when both of us have thought things through or when we aren't so affected by our emotions."

- "Broken Records"

This technique is useful to keep you from feeling trapped in a situation where other people might be trying to manipulate you. You can use what's known as a "broken record" by saying (whatever) firmly over and over. This lets you have a say without escalating conflict or retreating. Let's say you're arguing about money again with your partner. You could say, "It makes me feel frustrated when we don't agree about money." If they continue wanting to argue, you can just keep repeating, "It makes me feel frustrated when we don't agree about money."

- Show You Want Cooperation

When you can be inclusive, ask for other people's views, and be assertive, you'll achieve higher levels of cooperation from the people around you. Say, "Let's look at both the pros and cons of this...." or, "When would it be convenient to talk about this matter in more detail?"

- Ask to Be Understood

Never assume that everyone knows how their behavior or words affect you. Never assume that they're able to read your mind about the things you might want. Here are ways you can assertively voice your needs:

"I don't appreciate it when you (insert action.) Please stop it now."

"I don't like (insert whatever you don't like). I like (insert what you do like) better."

"I don't feel comfortable with this idea. The way I see it...."

"I'd like to go back to what happened this evening. It's important for me because...."

- Use the Word "And" Rather Than "But"

Using the word "and" rather than the word "but" might not seem natural or may even seem contradictory. However, making this change can create a sense of understanding and cooperation in situations where it might be hard for you to say "no."

You can use this technique if your boss asks you to stay late to work on a project when you've already scheduled an important evening out with your partner. Here's a scenario of how you could handle this:

Boss: "I need you to stay late and help with this project that's important for our department."

You: "I know this project is important for our department, AND I have to leave shortly to go to (your outing)."

Boss: "But you're the only person I truly trust with this project to get it done on time. If it doesn't get done, we're all going to be in trouble."

You: "Yes, I understand that this project is important, AND I really have to go to (your outing) this evening."

- Find Ways to Agree While Talking About Differences

If somebody expresses disapproval, you have to find something within their criticism that you actually agree with. Use their words to express your agreement with parts of their statement. This will show them that you've listened to them and heard them. Now you can clearly explain how your views are different and offer a solution. Look at this example:

"I respect your views. I do interpret what happened differently, though, because of (your view). Why don't we....?"

123

"You're spot on about the recent price increase. This is, however, out of my control. What I CAN do for you is...."

- A Different Way to Say "No, I Can't."

It's normal to get a request for help even if you're in the middle of working on something else. For some people, it might be hard or even impossible to say, "No, I can't."

Here's an alternative:

"I can't commit to this, as I have other priorities right now."

Adding this modification to a statement lets you temporarily delay responding to the request:

"I can't commit to this as I have other priorities right now. Let's touch base in one hour."

"Now isn't a good time because I'm in the middle of something. Why don't we reconnect at 3 pm?"

- Tell It the Way It Is

If somebody is pitching you their idea, trying to sell you something, or wants you to do or give them something that doesn't interest you, there are phrases you can use to tell them you're considering something else without offending them. By adding that you'll keep them in mind, it shows you're keeping the door open to discussions in the future.

For example:

"This doesn't meet my needs right now, but I'll be sure to keep you in mind."

"That won't work for me right now, but I'll get back to you if there are any changes."

"I really appreciate you thinking about me, but I've just got too much on my plate right now. I'll get back to you if anything changes."

Having assertiveness skills increases your confidence level while decreasing your stress level. There's a fine line between being thought of as assertive versus being aggressive. If you aren't sure whether you'll come across as aggressive or assertive, ask your friends, family, coworkers, etc., for their honest feedback.

The Importance of "No"

For those with a more permissive communication style, saying no can be a huge feat. However, research has shown that the more difficulty you have with saying no, the greater the chances of feeling stressed, depressed, and burned out. Saying no is a major game-changer. Anyone who feels stressed from being over-committed can benefit significantly from saying no.

If you're a person who likes to please others, saying no will be a tough challenge for you. However, it's important to remember that when expressing your needs and your feelings, there will be times when staying true to yourself involves saying no.

The following are some strategies to improve your ability to say no:

126

1. Figure out what your yes is.

Before you can get better at telling a person no, you need to understand the options implied in saying no to a particular thing. Every opportunity to pass on one thing is also an opportunity to say yes to something you'd rather do. It's a lot easier to say no when you know what you'll get to do instead. If agreeing to take part in the PTA fundraiser means you'll spend less time with your kids, focus on this fact to help you say no so you adhere to your priorities.

2. Try to sleep on it.

Even if you're thinking about saying yes, ask for a day to think about things before answering. It will be a lot easier to say no after you've taken the time to consider all your other commitments and whether the task you're considering can be realistically added to your schedule.

3. Try sandwiching your no.

You can make a no more palatable by sandwiching the no between two yeses. It also helps you explain what you've already committed yourself to. For example, if you're asked to work the weekend shift but you've already made commitments to your family that can't be broken, explain this to your boss. That's the first yes. Then tell your boss how these commitments will prevent you from working the weekend, which is the no. Complete your explanation by confirming your commitment to your job and business by asking if there's some other way to contribute that doesn't mean you have to work the weekend. This is the second yes.

4. Ensure that what you say is an actual no.

"No" is a powerful word that you shouldn't be afraid to use. When you need to say no, avoid phrases like, "I'm not certain," or, "I don't think I can." These limp phrases don't say no, and most people will assume you might be saying yes.

5. Get ready to repeat yourself.

Once you say no, the other party may push back, so the best thing to do is repeat yourself. This is often a lot easier to do when you can recognize the need beforehand. You may have to repeat yourself several times. If you provided them with any type of explanation with your first response, you could choose to repeat all of that again or simply say no. Don't allow them to back you into a corner of explaining yourself. You have the right to say no to anything you want.

When you say no to new commitments, you honor your existing commitments. This also gives you the chance to fulfill the commitments you have.

Verbal Traits

Passive

- Uses apologetic words and phrases such as "Sorry", "I am afraid", ...
- Creates a lot of ambiguity and uncertainty in the sentences delivered, emphasized by words such as, "possibly", "may be", "if possible", "perhaps" and "not sure".
- Ends sentences with an inflection making them seem a rhetorical question
- Brings themselves down in comparison to others by stating "I am not really good at this", "You obviously know more about this than I do", "I have never done this before", "It's my mistake really"

- Expects to need permission and may ask directly for this. For example, "Can I do this?", "Do you mind if I go ahead?" and "Is this OK with you?"
- Dismisses their own needs. For example, "It's OK, I should be alright"

Aggressive

- Uses accusatory phrasing in their language.
- Uses a lot of "I" statements. It is all about the person who is delivering the request.
- Uses threatening language. There can be many "if" statements which lead to punishment if the request is not satisfied. For example, "If you don't comply, I will ..."
- Delivers opinions as facts.
- Uses sarcasm and mockery.
- Uses forceful words such as "must", and "will" frequently.

Assertive

- Composes sentences logically.
- Thinks through the request and has an obvious solid structure to the reasoning.
- Uses clear and concise statements. The receiving end has no problem understanding what is wanted of them.
- Cares about the opinion of others and is willing to compromise as necessary to achieve the higher aim
- "I" statements are present but are used sparingly when appropriate.

CHAPTER 8: SETTING BOUNDARIES

Boundaries are a way for you to express what makes you comfortable or uncomfortable or what you'd like to happen or not happen within a relationship. Setting and maintaining boundaries is an essential part of being assertive in your relationships and taking care of yourself within those relationships. You shouldn't ignore your needs to satisfy the other person(s) in the relationship.

Dangers of Lacking Boundaries

Whether it's a physical boundary or a mental one, boundaries are meant to protect us. They aren't meant to limit our pleasure or to punish others. Enforcing and respecting physical and personal boundaries helps to protect us from environmental dangers, ourselves, and other people. It's a form of self-empowerment.

To set relational boundaries requires open communication in asserting your values to help protect those values from being compromised or violated. When you set healthy boundaries, you take care of and value yourself. Needing boundaries isn't uncaring, selfish, or mean. If another person gets upset because you set a boundary, that's on them, not you. You have every right and the responsibility to yourself to have healthy boundaries that protect you.

You have the right to have boundaries that match up with your moral compass and core values. Going against your values creates anxiety, loss of self-esteem and self-respect, and incongruency between your internal beliefs and your actions. Enforcement of firm boundaries and a healthy sense of self serve as preventive measures against being manipulated or allowing yourself to be at the mercy of emotionally needy people.

Emotionally needy people are often:

- Physically and emotionally draining
- Overly dramatic
- Self centered and selfish—only their problems, feelings, and ideas are important
- Abusive
- Invasive and pushy
- Smothering
- Critical
- Needing constant attention, praise, admiration, and reassurance
- Controlling
- Disrespectful of your time, self, and possessions
- Demanding

If you start to feel exhausted, angry, resentful, or mistreated when you're around a person, you might need to work on setting and enforcing stronger boundaries. One of the significant consequences of not doing so is the negative impact it tends to have on your relationships with others. When you lack boundaries

135

with one person, it can be detrimental to other important family, work, and social relationships. When you're overwhelmed by emotional fatigue, resentment, and anger, this increases the odds of those negative feelings being misdirected onto some undeserving individual.

When you don't have healthy boundaries, you're inviting others to disrespect you.

How to Set Boundaries

With that in mind, let's get into how to set healthy boundaries. The first thing you have to do is get clear with yourself. What is it that you need? It can be tricky to trust yourself about what your boundaries are, especially if you've never had people model this. That means you're going to have to get really honest with yourself about your wants and needs. It might be that you want a more positive relationship with your sibling, or you could be looking for more independence. The important thing is to prioritize your own needs.

A great way to do this is to write these things down.
136

Practice what's called a boundary circle. Start by drawing a circle in the middle of a piece of paper. Write down what you need to hear, see, and support inside the circle. On the outside of the circle, write the things that distract you.

Keep in mind that your boundaries can and will change over time. You have the power to set a boundary today and then alter or drop that boundary the next day. We're all on a journey, so we can't expect things to stay the same forever.

Once you have a good idea of what your boundaries are, start communicating them. This is the key to setting and maintaining them, especially if you're dealing with someone who consistently oversteps your boundaries. You don't have to make these moments confrontational, but you need to let people know exactly what your boundary is. You can't expect them to respect it if they aren't aware of it. For example, if you have a friend who's always sending you messages, say something like, "I see you want to get in touch with me, but the best thing is to send one message, and I'll write back when I can." This lets them know your boundary and gives them an alternative behavior.

Here are some steps you can take to communicate your boundaries to others:

1. Acknowledge – Starting a conversation with a statement of acknowledgment establishes the reality that you're setting or changing your boundaries and that this may be new behavior. These statements typically start with, "I know…" and may go something like this: " I know it's been hard as I've been reassessing my boundaries."

2. Explain – This is where you explain how you feel, typically using "I" statements.

3. Offer – When you share emotions, it's often done with the hope that the other person will be aware of what you want. When you provide an offer, this is where you state your boundary. This lets them know what you'd like from them.

If, after you take these steps, a person continues to disrespect your boundary, remind them of the boundary. In the end, if they continue to prove to you that they're not going to respect your boundaries, you may need to cease or lessen your contact with them.

For your boundaries to have a strong foundation, you need to show yourself some love. If you have an internal narrative that you're undeserving and worthless, you'll find it hard to keep the boundaries you set for yourself. It doesn't take a lot of work to encourage this type of mindset.

Creating boundaries means that both people will better understand their relationship and what each needs and expects from it. Learning to be assertive starts with knowing your boundaries. Being assertive and setting and maintaining your boundaries is about learning to communicate clearly and without anger or aggression what you mean and where your parameters lie. No one can read your mind, so you need to let people know your needs and expectations.

When setting boundaries, here are a few questions to ask yourself:

1. What behaviors have you allowed or participated in that compromised your wants and needs or violated your values?
2. How will this affect your relationship and you?
3. Will you put in the effort and risk to keep your boundaries?
4. Do you believe you have rights? What are these rights? What will your bottom line be?
5. What are some things you've done or said that haven't worked well for you and why?
6. Are there consequences that you're willing to live with? You must always mean what you say and never threaten something that you aren't willing to do. Keep in mind that any effort is undone if you can't keep your boundaries and enforce the consequences.
7. Will you be able to handle another person's reactions?

When it comes to setting and maintaining boundaries,

you have to take small steps, practice, get some support, practice, and, did I mention, practice? Think about this quote: "To maintain your limit over the long haul, you need to have the conviction that the limit is needed and appropriate. Conviction comes when you know how much it costs to not have the limit in place. The longer you wait, the more it costs."

What Setting Boundaries Means

You've probably heard people talk about setting boundaries, but do you know what this really means? According to clinical psychologist Dr. Carla Marie Manly, "Boundaries are the separations that humans need physically, emotionally, and mentally to feel safe, valued, and respected."

- You Have to Tell Others

Boundaries distinguish what makes us uncomfortable or comfortable, and usually, we convey this information using our voice. Use clear phrases to express your needs and comfort levels. For example, during this COVID pandemic, you could respectfully ask the people around you to wear a mask, stand a certain distance away from you, and wash their hands or use hand sanitizer before coming near you. Practicing this in your own home should lessen the discomfort when you're talking to your neighbors or other people in your community.

- It's Okay to Say "No"

This is a critical but challenging part of creating boundaries. You have to learn to say that tiny, two-letter word—"No." Most of the time, we feel we owe other people a page-long explanation about why we can't do something for them, go to a concert, or work longer. The truth is, good boundaries are explanations in and of themselves. You could say something like, "I'm sorry, but I can't commit to working on the project this weekend. I do appreciate that you thought of me and have confidence in me, but this weekend isn't good for me." This is a good response. No explanation is necessary.

- You Have to Be Transparent and Honest

Just making a conscious decision to set boundaries won't be enough. You have to communicate these boundaries to others. They don't have magic wands or telepathy to know what you do or don't want, so the only way they'll know is if you tell them.

- You Need to Know When to Tighten or Expand Boundaries

Anybody who has healthy boundaries will be able to adjust these boundaries depending on the situation to allow the right degree of connection for them. We unconsciously and consciously use boundaries to show others what's appropriate and acceptable. If these boundaries are too easily permeated, we develop a tendency to allow others to take advantage of us and accept their abusive treatment. If the boundaries are too strict, we might start behaving in a highly defensive manner to keep people at arm's length.

Setting Boundaries Is Healthy

Setting boundaries is important in finding your identity and is critical for your well-being and mental health. Boundaries might be emotional or physical, and they might range from rigid or loose. Most healthy boundaries fall in between these extremes.

Think back to your elementary school days. You can probably picture those huge maps that hung on the

143

wall that the teacher pulled down with a hook. Your teacher probably took a pointer and showed you the various lines that indicated the boundaries between countries and states. There might have been some features like lakes or rivers that divided one country or state from another, but, in most cases, lines were used. The funny thing about these boundaries is that when you travel, you don't see any definitive lines that separate one state or country from another. We just accept that they're there, and we know when we've crossed into a different state or country.

We seem to grasp this map concept of boundaries more easily than boundaries in our personal relationships. Unfortunately, most of the time, there aren't any physical or literal barriers between others and ourselves. But even if there are—think cubicles in an office—these boundaries rarely work. People will always find a way to cross that line one way or another.

This is why it's necessary to set emotional and personal boundaries. These are your way of letting others know how far they can push you with regard to matters like work, emotional support, or asking for advice or help—

and how often they can ask for these things.

In reality, boundaries can be difficult to identify and extremely tricky to set. This isn't anything like geography, and we didn't learn how to do it in school. Few of us were trained in setting them as a way of fostering healthy relationships in our lives.

To help you understand emotional and personal boundaries, how to set them, and how to stick with them, let's look at some examples.

Examples

To help you get a better idea of what boundaries are and how to set them, let's take a look at what healthy boundaries look like.

The first type of boundary is a physical boundary. This includes your needs for personal space, your comfort with being touched, and physical needs like water, food, and rest. You can tell people that you don't want to be touched or that you need some space. You can also tell others that you need rest or you're hungry.

145

Stating physical boundaries could sound like this:

- "Don't go into my room without asking."
- "No, I don't want you to touch me like that."
- "I'm allergic to (insert item), so we can't have that in our home."
- "I need to eat. I'm going to go grab something."
- "I would rather do a handshake. I'm not much of a hugger."

Then there are emotional boundaries. These are all about honoring and respecting energy and feelings. To set emotional boundaries, you have to recognize how much emotional energy you can take in, be aware of when you do and don't want to share, and limit emotional sharing with those who tend to respond badly. When emotional boundaries are respected, you validate the feelings of others and ensure that you respect their ability to take in emotional information. Stating emotional boundaries could sound like:

- "I really can't talk about that right now. It isn't the right time."

- "I'm having a hard time and really need to talk. Are you in a place to listen right now?"
- "I'm so sorry you're having a rough time. Right now, I'm not in a place to take in all this information. Do you think we can talk about this later?"

Thirdly, we have time boundaries. Time is a valuable commodity, so you have to know how to prioritize it. Time boundaries are extremely important socially, at home, and at work. Setting time boundaries means you understand what your priorities are and set aside the time you need so you don't over-commit yourself. Healthy time boundaries may sound like this:

- "I'm happy to help with that. My hourly rate is…"
- "We have family time on Sundays, so we won't be able to make it."
- "Do you have time to chat today?"
- "I can only stay an hour."
- "I can't make it this weekend, I have an event."

147

Since boundaries can help us feel more comfortable and safe, it makes perfect sense that these discussions about boundary issues often arise during therapy. Boundaries have a considerable impact on our mental well-being. Emotional boundaries are critical because they give us the personal space we need in any situation. If these boundaries are respected, we feel safe, honored, and valued. Boundaries can also help us heal. They help us not feel we're always being taken advantage of. Even though maintaining these boundaries might be difficult at times, doing so can increase our self-esteem and self-compassion by letting us prioritize our needs and voice.

Challenges

If you've repeatedly communicated your boundaries and it isn't working, it's probably because:

1. Your tone of voice isn't firm, or you might sound critical or blaming.
2. You don't enforce consequences when someone violates your boundaries.

3. You constantly back down if you're challenged with name-calling, threats, anger, or reason. You might go so far as to give them the "old silent treatment" or respond like this:
   a. "Stop trying to control me!"
   b. "That's so selfish of you."
   c. "Who do you think you are by telling me what to do?"

4. Your threats are too unrealistic or extreme to be believed. For example: "If you do that again, I'll leave."

5. You don't appreciate how important your values and needs are.

6. You never exercise consequences consistently each time a boundary is violated.

7. You easily back down since you have sympathy for another person's pain, and you put their feelings above yours.

8. You always insist that another person change. Consequences were never meant to punish or to try and change their behavior but to make you change your own behavior.

9. You don't have support systems in place to help you reinforce your behavior.

10. Your actions and words contradict each other. Actions will always speak louder. Any action that rewards somebody for violating your limits only proves that you were never serious. Here are a few examples:

   a. You tell your neighbor not to stop by without calling first, but then you let them into your house without being invited

   b. You tell your significant other "no contact," but then you see and text them anyway.

   c. You tell people not to call you after 9 pm, but you answer the phone when they call.

   d. You give attention that only reinforces bad behavior like complaining or nagging about the bad behavior but not taking any action. In the example above, when you tell someone not to call you, but they do and you answer the phone, you're reinforcing the bad behavior.

People who have low self-esteem or are co-dependent have difficulty setting boundaries because:

1. They have no idea what they feel or need.
2. Even if they do know these things, they don't value their wants, feelings, and needs, and they usually put other people's feelings and needs ahead of their own. They feel guilty and anxious when they ask for what they need or want.
3. They don't believe they have rights.
4. They're afraid they'll make someone angry or be judged by others.
5. They don't like feeling vulnerable. They feel ashamed if they show their true feelings or ask for something they want.
6. They're scared of losing a person's approval, friendship, or love.
7. They never want to be a burden.

If emotional boundaries aren't respected, it could leave you feeling anxious, bullied, and overwhelmed. If these boundaries are constantly disrespected, feelings of powerlessness and despair could trigger trauma, depression, and anxiety. You might begin feeling like a caged animal at the mercy of its caretaker when boundaries aren't respected.

CONCLUSION

Thank you for making it through to the end of *Assertiveness Training*. Let's hope it was informative and able to provide you with all the tools you need to achieve your goals, whatever they may be.

The next step is to start practicing assertiveness. That's the only way you'll be able to build this skill. You have to start using the strategies and techniques we've covered in this book to become a more assertive communicator. It won't be easy at first. Just think back to when you first learned your multiplication tables. You probably had difficulty learning that three times seven was 21, but the more you kept practicing, the easier it got. It's the same thing with being assertive. Practice makes perfect, as cliché as that might sound.

Additionally, we discussed the significance of setting strong boundaries. Boundaries are extremely important because they create the foundation for healthy relationships. If boundaries aren't established, you may become sad or angry because of interactions that cause you to feel you're being taken advantage of, bullied, unappreciated, or devalued.

Above all else, remember to value yourself. If you can't speak up for yourself, there's probably not another person who will do so. Sure, your parents, best friend, or partner may have your back, but, in the end, you need to be able to speak up for yourself. You don't have to be rude or make enemies in the process. Proper assertiveness won't do that. What it will do is make people respect you and, in the end, you'll respect yourself.

One more thing

If you enjoyed this book and found it helpful, I'd be very grateful if you'd post a short review on Amazon. Your support does make a difference, and I read all the reviews personally so I can get your feedback and make this book even better. I love hearing from my readers, and I'd really appreciate it if you leave your honest feedback.

Thank you for reading!

BONUS CHAPTER

I would like to share a sneak peek into another one of my books that I think you will enjoy. The book is titled ***"The Keys to Being Brilliantly Confident and More Assertive: A Vital Guide to Enhancing Your Communication Skills, Getting Rid of Anxiety, and Building Assertiveness."***

All of us can think of times when we know we should speak up, but we don't. When we feel like we're being taken advantage of, but we just accept it. Later, we kick ourselves, thinking: "If only I would have said something!"

If this sounds like you, look no further! This book serves as a complete guide to understanding assertiveness and becoming more assertive in your own life.

Using practical exercises and techniques, it will teach you how to stand up for what you believe in, ask for what you want, and say no to what you don't want in a way that's confident, calm, and respectful. This book will also show you how to increase your self-confidence and your self-worth.

This book is for:

- People who would like to massively boost their assertiveness
- People who would like to learn how to deal with conflicts
- People who would like to communicate with confidence and charisma
- New managers who need to be more assertive with their team.
- Emerging leaders who want to communicate more clearly and confidently.

- Introverted people who need to set boundaries and say "no."
- Passive communicators who want to speak more directly and honestly.
- People who have difficulty protecting their time, priorities, and goals.
- People who need to set stronger boundaries.
- People who are tired of being a doormat and taking a passive role in relationships
- People who are afraid of standing up for themselves
- People who are tired of being controlled and dominated
- People who struggle with knowing their worth.

This book will teach you the following:
- How to be an Assertive Communicator
- How to Communicate with Confidence and Charisma
- Highly Effective Techniques to Deal with Any Conflict in Your Personal & Professional Life

- How to Have an Assertive Body Language
- How to Speak Up, Share Your Ideas & Opinions in A Persuasive, Calm & Positive Way
- How to Say "no" and establish boundaries without Looking Selfish
- How to Reduce Discomfort When Talking to People
- How to Overcome your fears and limiting beliefs about being assertive
- How to better manage conflict and difficult conversations

Learning how to be more assertive can massively improve your relationships and your overall sense of self-confidence. When you can express yourself assertively and speak up for yourself, other people will respect you more. Even more importantly, you will respect yourself more. Once you start improving your assertiveness, incredible things will happen in your life.

Enjoy this free chapter!

160

All of us can think of times when we know we should speak up, but we don't. When we feel like we're being taken advantage of, but we just accept it. Later, we kick ourselves, thinking: "If only I would have *said something!*"

This book will help you if you are a person who feels like you need to increase your assertiveness, to improve your communication skills, to better deal with conflict, to improve your level of confidence and to be a better leader. In this book, you will learn how to improve all of these skills and more!

The purpose of this book is to serve as a complete guide to help you understand what assertiveness is and how you can become more assertive in your own life. Using practical exercises and techniques will teach you how to stand up for what you believe, ask for what you want and need, and say no to what you don't want in a way that's confident, calm, and respectful. This book will also be your guide for increasing self-confidence and self-worth. By reading this book, you will improve your life, gain more control over your life, improve your communication skills and your interpersonal skills and be more successful in both your personal life and your work life.

Before we begin delving into how you can start to take action, we are going to look at an important theory related to changing oneself. This theory comes down to your mindset. The type of mindset that you employ has a massive impact on your life and your growth as a person. There is something called a Growth Mindset, which is an essential piece of this book and your goals of changing yourself. The **'growth mindset'** is a term that was coined by Carol Dweck, who is a renowned professor at multiple universities, including Columbia University, Harvard University, and the University of Illinois. Her research with Angela Lee Duckworth stated that intelligence is not a key indicator of success. They believed that success depends on whether or not a person has a *growth mindset*. A **'fixed mindset'** is the opposite of a growth mindset. A fixed mindset is a term for when a person believes that their intelligence and skills are fixed traits and that they are not able to be changed. People of this mindset believe that they have what they have, and that's it.

Knowing this fact and the proof it provides can help you to feel empowered and hopeful. If you struggle with your confidence and your level of assertiveness, understanding that it is a skill that can be learned and honed over time means that this will not remain something that you struggle with anymore. By picking up this book, you are already taking the first steps involved in changing your life by becoming a more confident and more assertive person. If this were an innate characteristic, this would mean that it would be difficult for you to change. Take comfort in this fact and continue reading this book as we will discuss exactly how you can make these changes in your life.

By the end of this book, you will be well on your way to changing your life for the better in numerous ways, and you will be wondering how you ever lived without this information. There is no better time than now to change the parts of yourself that you wish were different.

What Does It Mean to Be Assertive?

To begin, we are going to look at what assertiveness is,

as well as some points related to assertiveness so that you can get a better idea of what exactly this word means. By first making sure that you understand assertiveness, this will help you to understand what benefits can come of assertiveness and how it will benefit you.

What Is Assertiveness?

Assertiveness is being able to use effective communication as well as negotiation, in order to remain true to your personal needs and boundaries when interacting with other people. Being assertive isn't about aggressively putting up walls and shutting people out, contrary to popular belief. There is no shame in being assertive; it is quite a valued skill both in a person's personal life and in their work or professional life.

Assertiveness Is a Skill, Not a Personality Trait

Assertiveness, communication, conflict resolution, confidence, and leadership. What do all of these have in common? All of these are skills and not innate characteristics. What does this mean? I will start by defining these two terms for you. A learned skill, as I am sure you can imagine, is something that you can learn and develop in order to possess. This is the opposite of an innate characteristic, which is something that you are born with. For instance, the color of your eyes or certain aspects of your personality, such as being stubborn.

Skills are things that you can study, practice, and improve upon. Skills are things like communication or cooking. On the other hand, a characteristic is something that you possess that you do not have much control over. You can work on things like becoming less stubborn, but for the most part, you are born a stubborn person, or you are not.

Remember, in the introduction to this book when we discussed the differences between a *fixed mindset* and a *growth mindset*? This comes into play here once again, as you must check your mindset before setting out to make changes. Having a fixed mindset makes a person highly concerned with what skills and intelligence they currently have, and those that they were born with, and it does not allow them any room to focus on what they can develop or improve upon. Therefore, their activities are limited to the capacity that they think they have.

However, those with growth mindsets understand that skills and intelligence are something that can be developed and learned throughout the course of their life. This can be done through reading, education, training, mentorships, or simply just passion. They understand that their brain is a muscle that can be 'worked out' to grow stronger. Knowing this, you must employ a growth mindset. Every single skill you have, as well as your intelligence and confidence, can be improved or changed by putting in the effort to do so. Famous public figures of success like Oprah Winfrey, Steve Jobs, and Bill Gates all employed a growth mindset, which allowed them to overcome every obstacle that got in their way. Rather than succumbing to defeat, they worked and discovered innovative ways to overcome previous failures and found success at the end.

Think about what mindset you have right now. If you

already have a growth mindset, you simply need to continue practicing it while being proactive about dealing with obstacles and overcoming failures. If you think you are someone with a fixed mindset, you must change it right now. Believe me when I tell you that confidence and skills such as assertiveness can be improved upon with time and hard work, and this book will show you how. If you don't believe me, just try it. Pick a random skill; this could be knitting, computer programming, jogging, or anything that can be learned. Set goals for yourself and begin learning something new. If you can take something that you have zero skill in and become proficient in it, you have just proved to yourself that growth mindsets are real and fixed mindsets only hold you back from success. This is proof that the only thing holding you back from becoming a more assertive and confident you, is your mindset.

Take some time to consider this and evaluate yourself and your mindset before moving on, as it will play a vital part in your success throughout this book and life.

The Benefits of Assertiveness

167

There are numerous benefits to assertiveness, many of which you are likely aware of, or you would not have opened this book in the first place. In this section, we will look at some of the most valuable benefits of being an assertive person.

- Being assertive allows you to communicate in a confident and clear way
- Being assertive allows you to practice self-care by setting boundaries and sticking to them
- Being assertive allows you to deal with conflict in your personal and professional lives most effectively and maturely possible
- Being assertive allows you to share your ideas and thoughts persuasively and calmly, which will command attention and respect
- Being assertive allows you to ensure your needs are being met
- Being assertive allows you to feel comfortable and confident, saying "no."
- Being assertive helps you to provide feedback to others in a constructive and effective way
- Being assertive improves your interpersonal skills

- Being assertive helps you to be more confident in yourself and your decisions and ideas
- Being assertive helps you to reduce your stress levels by helping you to confidently prioritize your time and energy
- Being assertive increases your self-respect, self-confidence, and self-worth
- Being assertive helps you to be a better negotiator
- Being assertive helps you to remain calm under pressure

Why Many People Struggle With Assertiveness

One of the main reasons that people struggle with being assertive is because it is a means to protect oneself. A person may not even realize that they are doing this to protect themselves, and they may genuinely want to be more assertive. Still, many people have trouble with this because the avoidance of being assertive helps a person feel as though they are in control of their life by avoiding the possibility of negative emotions. This is what is called a defensive measure. Defensive measures are actions that a person takes to avoid getting hurt or to minimize the risk of getting hurt. External defensive behaviors are a type of defensive measure that is used to help a person prevent harm or conflict with other people. This includes being non-assertive, being submissive, silencing yourself, blaming yourself, and keeping distance between yourself and others. This is a common reason that people have a lack of assertiveness, and it is something that we will address heavily in this book.

Behind this effort to avoid getting hurt, there could be many reasons. The most common reasons begin in childhood, believe it or not. Our upbringing and childhood experiences typically play a massive role in your level of self-esteem in your adult life. Did you grow up in a strict family who barely ever gave you praise? Did a more successful sibling always overshadow you? Did you grow up in a family where nobody was ever around, and you were left to fend for yourself? These are all examples and reasons why people may have lower self-esteem compared to others. Studies show that children who were raised in families or households where love was not often shown or expressed, typically had lower levels of self-esteem later in life when compared to children that were shown love or who grew up in families where love was expressed.

Further, in an incredibly fast-paced society with the obsessive usage of social media, it is so difficult not to compare ourselves to others. Have you ever found yourself obsessively stalking or following a celebrity's Instagram page? Are you continually following people who became millionaires at the ripe age of 22? Or are you following gorgeous models who have the world's population fiending for them? In this day and age, our exposure to hotter, wealthier, and more successful people are continuously growing. Seeing incredible success like this every day really makes it hard for you to recognize your self-worth and, in turn, lowers your self-esteem.

How Assertiveness Is Linked to Self-Esteem

When people have a healthy level of self-esteem, they typically have a positive outlook on themselves. They believe in their capabilities to achieve goals and do not spend a lot of time dwelling on failure. They are not afraid to ask for help from others to help them reach their goals. They are also able to be assertive and be able to say "no" to situations or requests that they do not want to do.

Having a healthy level of self-esteem helps increase assertiveness because you believe in what you are saying and doing. If you believe that you need or want something, you won't spend time dwelling on whether you think other people think it is true, you will just ask for it. Those who have low self-esteem typically suffer from not being able to ask for what they need or want because they are afraid of being judged or rejected. In their minds, asking for something for 'need' is a sign of weakness, and therefore, people will judge them for asking for it. On the flip side, somebody with a healthy level of self-esteem typically isn't afraid of that because that hasn't even crossed their mind. Since having healthy self-esteem comes from loving yourself and respecting yourself, it feels perfectly reasonable to ask for what they feel like they need and want.

For this reason, self-esteem and assertiveness are inextricably linked, and to work on one, we must work on the other. Throughout this book, you will see how self-esteem and assertiveness play into one another and how they come together in many different situations.

To help you understand further what being assertive means, I will provide you with an example. Imagine if your mother wanted you to come over to her house as soon as possible so you can help her pack up her things to prepare for a move. However, you had planned to spend your evening relaxing, watching a movie, and taking a hot bubble bath because you have had a busy week at work. Assertiveness, in this case, would be valuing your own needs just as much as you value your mother's needs. A person with a healthy amount of self-esteem will be able to demonstrate assertiveness by saying, "I am worthy of this. I deserve my break when I need it." Somebody with low self-esteem will typically think, "It will be selfish of me to take a break when somebody needs my help." A part of having self-esteem is being able to understand that you can't pour from an empty glass. In the example above, those with low self-esteem will go and help their mother move anyway despite being exhausted and end up feeling like other people do not respect their time and feelings. In reality, people do not know what you need if you are unable to communicate it. In the next chapter, we are going to look at communication styles and the most effective styles for being assertive and expressing yourself clearly.

Get your full copy today! *"The Keys to Being Brilliantly Confident and More Assertive: A Vital Guide to Enhancing Your Communication Skills, Getting Rid of Anxiety, and Building Assertiveness."*

BOOKS BY RICHARD BANKS

How to be Charismatic, Develop Confidence, and
Exude Leadership: The Miracle Formula for Magnetic
Charisma, Defeating Anxiety, and Winning at
Communication

How to Stop Being Negative, Angry, and Mean:
Master Your Mind and Take Control of Your Life

How to Deal with Grief, Loss, and Death: A Survivor's
Guide to Coping with Pain and Trauma, and Learning
to Live Again

How to Deal With Stress, Depression, and Anxiety: A
Vital Guide on How to Deal with Nerves and Coping
with Stress, Pain, OCD and Trauma

The Positive Guide to Anger Management: The Most
Practical Guide on How to Be Calmer, Learn to Defeat
Anger, Deal with Angry People, and Living a Life of

Mental Wellness and Positivity

Develop a Positive Mindset and Attract the Life of Your Dreams: Unleash Positive Thinking to Achieve Unbound Happiness, Health, and Success

The Keys to Being Brilliantly Confident and More Assertive: A Vital Guide to Enhancing Your Communication Skills, Getting Rid of Anxiety, and Building Assertiveness

Generalized Anxiety Disorder: The Universal Formula for Managing Stress, Building Your Self-Esteem and Self-Confidence, and Achieving Superior Mental Wellness

Sober for Life: The Most Effective Guide on How to Achieve Sobriety, Ridding Oneself of Alcoholism, and Learning to Rebuild a Life of Wellness, Alcohol-Free